"I'm Here Waiting":
Birth Relatives' Views on Part II of the Adoption Contact Register for England and Wales

Note about the authors

Audrey Mullender is Professor of Social Work at the University of Warwick. During the period of the research project reported on here, she was Director of the Centre for Applied Social Studies at the University of Durham.

Sarah Kearn was Research Assistant to the project at the University of Durham.

"I'm Here Waiting"

Birth relatives' views on Part II of the Adoption Contact Register for England and Wales

Audrey Mullender and Sarah Kearn

British
Agencies
for **A**doption
and **F**ostering

Published by
British Agencies for Adoption & Fostering
(BAAF)
Skyline House
200 Union Street
London SE1 0LX

Charity registration 275689

British Library Cataloguing in Publication Data
A catalogue record for this book is available from the British Library

ISBN 1 873868 41 3

Designed by Andrew Haig & Associates
Cover illustration by Andrew Haig
Typeset by Avon Dataset Ltd, Bidford on Avon
Printed by Russell Press Ltd. (TU), Nottingham

To those who search
and research –
may they find what
they seek.

Acknowledgements

We gratefully acknowledge the support we received from the Nuffield Foundation in funding this project, the staff of the Office of National Statistics (ONS) (formerly OPCS, Office of Population and Census Surveys), the Adoptions Section at Southport in undertaking a major administrative task on our behalf, from all the members of the Advisory Group for their time and enormously useful advice, and from the University of Durham.

We also wish to thank all those who sent back questionnaires and also those who thought about doing so but knew it was not the right thing for them at this time. We recognise that being contacted about this research will have brought back painful memories for many people and that it took courage and generosity of spirit even to think about being involved. We hope that it will prove to have been worthwhile, in continuing to raise the profile of birth relatives of adopted people in relation to law and practice in England and Wales.

Audrey Mullender
Sarah Kearn

Contents

	Introduction	1
1.	**The social and historical background to the study**	3
2.	**The contemporary legal situation after adoption and research on its impact**	24
3.	**Methodology of the research**	49
4.	**First impressions of the Adoption Contact Register**	70
5.	**The decision to register**	92
6.	**Outcomes of involvement with the Register**	103
7.	**Potential changes in the operation of the Register**	116
8.	**Relatives' views on openness in adoption**	134
9.	**New thoughts on "other relatives"**	141
10.	**A comparison between the contact registers available in Great Britain**	151
11.	**Conclusion**	159
	Appendix I	162
	Appendix II	168
	Appendix III	170
	Appendix IV	180
	Appendix V	181
	References	182

Introduction

This research project was concerned with investigating the use of Part II of the Adoption Contact Register for England and Wales since its establishment in May 1991, and in obtaining users' views of its manner of functioning and effectiveness in meeting their needs. The users of the Register are those birth relatives of adopted people who have signalled their willingness to be contacted by entering their details on the Register. Until recently – and still in most cases – birth relatives of adopted people have been 'an entirely anonymous, faceless part of society' (Post-Adoption Centre, 1990b, p. 1, describing birth parents). It has therefore been a privilege to be able to obtain access to the views of almost 2,000 relatives for the purposes of this research.

In order to understand the general implications of the establishment of the Adoption Contact Register, and respondents' views on its functioning, it is necessary to set the Register within its national and international context, in social, historical and legal terms.

It is a particularly timely moment to be so doing, in a period when the media has been concerned with a number of high profile cases involving women's current access to abortion, allegedly "on demand", and when the question has been revived as to whether the placement of babies for adoption might not be a realistic alternative (for example, on the *Today* programme on BBC Radio 4 on Monday 26 August 1996, which made the connection between approximately 160,000 abortions a year and only a few hundred baby adoptions). Yet there is now a considerable literature and a growing body of research concerning the adverse impact of placement for adoption on birth relatives, in particular on the mental health of birth mothers. This book will add to that body of work, and may be useful in informing the debate as to the likely personal and social costs of encouraging any return to a greater use of adoption. At the same time as these major social questions have been raised, a draft

Adoption Bill (Department of Health and Welsh Office, 1996) has been published. The consultation period ended on 28 June 1996. It was decided not to introduce adoption legislation during the final session of the last Parliament or the first session of the new Parliament, leaving both major parties to consider either manifesto commitments or less public intentions in this sphere. There has been no new Act for more than twenty years and the range of issues now requiring attention extends from routine regularisation to consideration of the whole role of adoption in future family policy. Post-adoption matters appear to have been submerged under the weight of these other considerations and, arguably, would merit their own separate attention in the law. Once again, this book would hope to influence the debate.

1 The social and historical background to the study

The social and legal origins of contemporary adoption

England and Wales can date their first statute on adoption to 1926. This was late in comparison with various states of the USA (beginning with Massachusetts in 1851), Australia, New Zealand and parts of Canada, and was not the first in Europe where Sweden had such a statute in 1918. Prior to that, there were simply *de facto* arrangements which gave a child's new carers no defensible rights in respect of him or her, and the child no comparable security, but which, on the other hand, did not break previously existing family ties. An adoption order afforded the child a legal status as if born to the adopters and, conversely, ended all legal relationship to the birth parents and their families. There are estimated currently to be around 750,000 adopted people in Britain (Post-Adoption Centre, 1990b, p. 1). They encompass both those for whom an adoption agency or a third party found adoptive parents, and also situations where a parent and step-parent, or other relatives, used adoption to obtain parental status in respect of the child. (For the purposes of this study, the latter groups are of less relevance since they tend not to carry the same connotations of the adopted person losing touch with his or her entire birth family as do adoptions by people who were formerly strangers to the child.)

From the late 1950s until 1967, a changing social climate saw a continuous rise in what were then heavily stigmatised as "illegitimate" births, and adoption orders peaked in 1968, with 15,613 non-parental adoptions; around 90 per cent involved "illegitimate" children (Grey, 1971). From then onwards, the advent of a wider choice and greater availability of contraceptive methods (notably the Pill) and abortion (legalised in 1967), together with increasing social acceptance and financial support for single mothers wanting to keep their babies, combined to reduce both unwanted pregnancies and adoptions. In other words, the freeing up of sexual mores was only belatedly accompanied by social and medical routes to lessening the stress and often despair which had faced those young women who found themselves pregnant in the 1950s and 60s. Many of the latter, who gave birth during the peak years for the adoption of babies, are among the birth mothers who now form the largest group using Part II of the Adoption Contact Register. Some birth mothers are, of course, considerably older, and there are also relatives of many other degrees of relationship on the Register. However, all can be argued to have been affected by the attitudes which have prevailed over the years towards women having children outside marriage, since these are the attitudes which have also shaped adoption.

The conditions which encouraged the intense feelings of shame and guilt a birth mother faced in the past, and the accompanying social and family pressures upon her to relinquish her child, were socially constructed – even though they were played out as private dramas marked by parental outrage or grief, fear of the neighbours, and women disappearing from view until after their confinements, and even though the women concerned had no idea at the time how many others were undergoing similar experiences. There is a close relationship between a society's stance towards, and handling of, unmarried motherhood, on the one hand, and its view and use of adoption, on the other (Howe *et al*, 1992). We were reminded of this afresh recently, on the day the Adoption Bill (Department of Health and Welsh Office, 1996) was issued for consultation, when a Conservative Government minister spoke in terms of ensuring that young single women becoming pregnant should be encouraged to think of adoption as a real choice. More recently, too, a speech by the then Prime Minister immediately before Christmas 1996 presented adoption as an unproblematic and desirable solution to various social ills.

This reflects the traditional Western model of adoption, affirming the assumed desirability of the two-parent family over lone mothers – the latter politically perceived not only as inadequate but also (in a return to the values of the Poor Law: Howe *et al*, 1992, pp. 6–8) as a burden on the state. Changing views of women's role in society and women's own claiming of a right to choose in relation to fertility, child-bearing and child-rearing (at least in dominant British society – cultural and religious factors can still strongly impinge), together with a proliferation of different types of family structure, may give an archaic air to imputations that births outside marriage represent irresponsible female sexuality (men having always been differently regarded). Nevertheless, large numbers of birth relatives of adopted people continue to live with the legacy of a time when this was not only the accepted but virtually the unquestioned view. Many have no doubt felt the full irony of a politics which harks back to that stance. A major underlying theme of this book will be the extent to which society and its legislators are willing to enhance their recognition of, and response to, the needs of those birth relatives.

Opening up adoption

Babies placed in the era described above were placed into "closed" adoption, that is, the birth relatives were not told who had adopted the baby or where they lived, and the adopters had no identifying information about the birth relatives. Identities were concealed by complete confidentiality in court proceedings, and the Registrar General's records were (to borrow from American terminology) "sealed", with the issuing of an adoption certificate to be used in place of the original birth certificate. There was then an impermeable boundary placed between access to the child's birth record in the Register of Births, only possible for those knowing the child's original identity, and access to the entry in the Adopted Children Register, only feasible for those knowing the new adoptive identity. (The short version of the new certificate makes no mention of the fact of adoption, so an adopted person who has one of these may not know they are adopted; needing a copy of the full certificate for some official purpose was a common way of finding out in former days.) The Registrar General keeps a record of, and can trace, the connection between entries in the Register of Births (now known as a "register of live-births") and corresponding entries in the Adopted Children Register, but may not make this public. (Technically, Griffith, 1991b, sec. 16, p. 8, refers to these as 'restricted access' rather than 'sealed' records since Section 50(5) does state that a court order can be made to furnish someone with the information. This has been tested in the High Court and it is notable that Section 62(4) of the draft

Adoption Bill 1996, will, if made law, allow the court this discretion only in "exceptional circumstances" which will not cover a normal desire for contact, however strongly felt.) A similar, social "sealing" took place when birth mothers encountered total silence about the events of their pregnancy and childbirth, shrouded throughout in secrecy and disgrace, or when they were continually told to put the episode behind them and resume their lives – as if the child had never been born.

Latterly, adoption practice has begun to move away from this "closed" approach. Firstly, it was recognised that children needed to know they were adopted and adopters began to be encouraged to talk about the background to the placement, though they would still not know or reveal birth family identities. A seminal piece of research by John Triseliotis (1973) led directly to a change in the law, when Section 26 of the Children Act 1975 gave people of 18 and over, who had been adopted in England and Wales, access to their birth records. Triseliotis had interviewed 70 adopted people who had acquired their birth records under Scottish law and had concluded that it was a normal psychosocial need for adopted people to want to know about their origins in order to develop a positive sense of identity. (Interestingly, most people in that study wanted equal rights for themselves *and* their birth parents, although this equity has not followed in the law.) Researchers who were then able to study adult adoptees obtaining birth records in England and Wales included Day (1979), Leeding (1980), and Haimes and Timms (1985). Haimes and Timms reconfirmed that the need of a young person to know his or her own life story was the norm, not the result of psychopathology or any element of failure in the adoption. Those adopted people who held back from tracing their birth families were, in the main, concerned not to hurt or deceive their adoptive parents. A further Scottish study was undertaken by Lambert *et al* in 1992, with similar results.

Latterly, the use of adoption for older children who have memories of family members has brought information exchange and/or continuing contact *throughout* childhood, not just at the age of 18 or over, onto the agenda. Even in infant adoptions, the widescale dissemination of knowledge about more open practices elsewhere has shifted the norm in this country to encompass, typically, a meeting between the birth mother and the prospective adopters before or at the time of placement, with an exchange of letters and photographs thereafter through the medium of the adoption agency acting as a "letterbox". It would still be rare in this country, following the placement of a baby or young child, for direct contact to continue through the parties knowing of one another's whereabouts, though this is the norm in New Zealand and, ironically, is easier to achieve in infant placements than in contested hearings concerning older children who may themselves have competing needs.

Much of the literature which has influenced practice in Britain in fact relates to the situation in New Zealand. (For instance, Iwanek, 1987; Dominick, 1988; Rockel and Ryburn, 1988; Fratter, 1991 and Mullender, 1991c all provide studies or accounts of open placements working well there.) There is also well-known material from Australia (Winkler and van Keppel, 1984) and the USA (Rillera and Kaplan, 1985; Lindsay, 1987).

A simple definition of open adoption is provided in a video made by a New Zealand adoption agency, Catholic Social Services (1985), which refers to it as 'a mutual agreement between the adoptive parents and the birth parents . . . that there'll be some form of continuing contact between them for the sake of the adopted child . . . an agreement that can be negotiated'. This context of mutuality and negotiation offers great flexibility to 'take account of changing needs and circumstances' (Ryburn, 1994b, p. 3). The definition refers to a model of complete openness – where birth and adoptive families spend time together as and when desired, under the control of the parties involved and with no mediation by the adoption agency. Noted academics in the adoption field in Britain have offered definitions and categorisations of openness which reflect the more complex situation pertaining in this country, and also internationally. Triseliotis (1991), for example, posits three models: "open adoption" of infants in New Zealand and through private agencies in some states of the USA, where the birth mother selects and meets the adopters, and they may remain in touch; "semi-open adoption" with involvement in selection but no meeting (or in the typical British variation involving one meeting at, or prior to placement, but with no exchange of disclosing information); and "adoption with contact" where an older or disabled child is found adopters who are comfortable to sustain his or her significant links. (This terminology has not passed into agreed usage.)

In the USA, openness can tend to be associated with a consumerist model of choice between different available "products" in the adoption field, both for the more informed birth mother or those advising her, and for prospective adopters. Rillera and Kaplan (1985) offer a handbook which explains how to arrive at "co-operative adoption" – proposed as the model of choice for those who favour a continuing relationship and interaction with one another as best for all parties (p. 110), including the adopted child. Addressing birth mothers, Lindsay (1987) argues that, just as no one would hire a babysitter without knowing something about the person (p. 21), so open adoption offers a real choice to women who do not feel ready for the responsibilities of motherhood, yet who do not wish to lose touch with their child and who want to be involved in choosing the prospective adopters for themselves. This can go beyond the New Zealand practice (also spreading in Britain) of selecting adopters from personal profiles they have prepared, complete with photographs, to interviewing several aspirant couples (p. 22). Lindsay reviews the evolution of openness in North America and describes the detailed practice of several named agencies which offer different degrees of openness. Her book is not without a certain crusading zeal in favour of adoption, including as a solution to what the writer of the Foreword sees as a serious social problem of "teen pregnancies". The "consumerist" element in the USA, where some states have not outlawed private or independent placements, can extend to adopters paying fees to register with an agency and also paying the birth mother's medical expenses associated with the birth. The 1989 BBC "40 Minutes" programme *Who'll win Jeanette?* showed a birth mother choosing between three couples, each of whom had paid a fee in the region of £900, and then becoming very close to the prospective adoptive mother – which may have had both a positive and a negative impact on her ability freely to finalise her decision to relinquish her child.

As well as influences between nations, there have also been belated but eventually positive influences between cultures over recent years. In adoption placement practice, there has been a clear link between indigenous or minority ethnic values which have always stressed care by the wider family or community, and the move away from traditional, closed adoption. Adoption of Aboriginal children in some of the Australian states, and of First Nations children in some provinces of Canada, for example, is within the family or keeps family members involved, even where this is not the norm. In South Australia, adoption of Aboriginal children only occurs at all if a guardianship agreement is not possible. In New Zealand, Maori child-rearing ideas, based on the responsibility and right of family and tribal groupings to make decisions about how best to care for children (currently being diluted in the UK into "family decision-making"), have influenced the whole of child care legislation and practice and have been enshrined in the Children, Young Persons and their Families Act 1989. They have undoubtedly assisted in the realisation that the total separation of the child from the family of origin, through adoption, was a relatively recent notion, imported from Europe, and represented a harmful loss of access to others who could provide love and concern as well as knowledge of family and cultural heritage. In Britain, closed adoption by strangers within small, nuclear family structures has been equally alien to black communities rooted in African, African-Caribbean or South Asian child-rearing practices and ideals. Child care practice in Britain, and in Australia and New Zealand owing to colonial influence, is facing up to the fact that it had a history of routinely removing black children to white families, initially because the latter were considered to provide innately superior care and, later, as a result of a lack of the skills and awareness needed to keep black children with their own families or to recruit black families to care for them. Thus, the imposition of closed adoption practice also represented the imposition of racist assumptions. Although black children in white families were openly, i.e. visibly, of adoptive status (Mallows, 1991), they were often not in touch with their immediate or extended birth families. Opening up adoption may therefore assist in challenging racial and cultural, as well as gender power structures, and in meeting children's cultural needs more effectively.

Continuing debate

Although adoption practice has now irrevocably opened up, professional social work opinion in Britain currently remains divided as to how far and how fast this should proceed. The more sceptical observers feel that the push for openness has ignored some of the complexities of the needs of individual children and of individual adoptive situations, particularly in the British context where increasing numbers of children are being adopted at an older age, often from local authority care following negative experiences with their birth families. Practitioners counselling caution include Kaniuk (1993) and Stogdon and Hall (1993). Ryburn (1994b), stemming from his own practice experience in New Zealand and research here, stands at the opposite pole, as the complete enthusiast for openness, and argues its value even where the adoption is contested (Ryburn, 1994a).

Much revolves around what are seen to be the needs of each member of the adoption "triangle" or "triad" – child, adopters and birth family – and what is regarded as the most desirable balance between their interests. Those who support openness most firmly argue that it works to the advantage of all parties because it answers awkward questions, provides the child with a sense of continuity and heritage, prevents the severing of valuable links of blood and affinity, and allows the birth parents to reassure the adoptive parents in their role whilst also meeting their own desire for information and contact. The more cautious, on the other hand, contend that adopters could not cope with openness, that contact would not prevent the birth relatives from having to cope with loss, and/or that the child could face conflicting loyalties or identity confusion, or would have less security than adoption requires to make it successful, or could face danger from previously abusive parents.

There are clear parallels with the ambivalent practice which continues to surround the maintenance of links between children in the public care and their families, despite twenty years of academic backing for its benefits (Thorpe, 1974, 1980; Millham *et al*, 1986; Harrison and Pavlovic, 1996). Nor are the problems any greater than those facing women who divorce men who have abused them and/or their children, yet women in that situation receive little support if they seek to refuse contact, even when the danger remains at its most acute (Hester and Radford, 1996). Furthermore, under the Children Act 1989, social workers (and foster carers) now have to work in partnership with even the most difficult parents regarding the care of their children. Stogdon and Hall consider it inappropriate to make comparisons with care or divorce cases since adoption is 'a necessary but unnatural contrivance' and, presumably, need not be required to cope with difficulties which are unavoidable where birth parents are still involved. This is a somewhat circular argument, in fact, given that all three concepts are socio-legally constructed and could be made to encompass or exclude contact according to prevailing ideological values. The unanswered questions remain the reasons for the ideological disparities between the different forms of family care for children. For instance, why do courts work from an assumption of contact in one form of decision-making regarding children (post-divorce) but still require convincing of its appropriateness in adoption? Why is parental dangerousness far less considered in the former case than the latter, despite statistical probabilities? And why are birth parents not spoken of as partners with the authorities in adoption as elsewhere in child care? There is scope, in fact, for a re-examination of the whole question of maintaining family links in every area of family law, together with the degree of risk (and to whom or what) which would make it proper to set these links aside, and the extent to which this is actually possible, given that feelings of belongingness may persist even when physical contact is denied. This rethinking also needs to bear in mind complexities such as gender (for example, the greater risks of sexual abuse from men), age (for example, the protection of the young, the age at which attachments and memories are formed), "race" and culture (for example, differing family structures, child-rearing practices, and emphases on the importance of family), and degree of relationship (since, for example, the needs and strengths of members of the extended family network have barely begun to be recognised). In the meantime, confusion persists in social work and judicial attitudes towards the birth parents of older children who are being adopted.

Contemporary work with birth mothers placing babies may no longer be marked by a punitive approach (though media and political views of birth mothers can still be negative in the extreme), but it does continue to vary as approaches to degrees of openness vary. Cooper (1993), reflecting on the different levels of counselling and consultation offered to birth mothers by adoption agencies prior to placement, notes this, with more or less marked moves towards allowing a birth mother a say in who adopts and keeping adoption records updated so as to facilitate contact at a later date. However, Cooper found birth mothers to be sceptical about the possibility of formalising contact prior to adoption, wondering who would ensure that any arrangement was followed through should adopters renege on the agreement. Clearly, this relates also to practice in selecting adoptive parents who are willing and able to be more inclusive of birth relatives. Indeed, arguments that adopters may struggle with openness are circular, in so far as adopters offer largely what they are recruited and selected to offer. In New Zealand, the preparation process for prospective adopters (still, predominantly, of babies) is premised on openness and may include an opportunity to meet a birth mother who can challenge any stereotypical thinking about birth mothers as responsible for their own misfortunes, or as selfish or disruptive. As one British birth mother said to Cooper: 'We're people, not machines. And we are mothers. Even if they don't like to see us that way' (p. 22). At the other extreme, a small number of birth mothers will continue to choose the absolute confidentiality of closed adoption without meeting the adopters, for example, some young Asian women who fear dishonour in their family and community (Vyas, 1993, p. 65).

The impact of closed adoption on birth relatives

Whatever the merits or demerits of open placements, and whatever the likelihood that they will continue to grow in number and in degree of openness in the future, they were unheard of when the majority of participants in the present study were losing their children, grandchildren, brothers, sisters, or other relatives to adoption. It is therefore relevant to look at what is known from research about the impact of closed adoption on birth mothers and other relatives.

Birth mothers

A number of studies, together with autobiographical, activist and more journalistic collections of first-hand accounts (for example, Shawyer, 1979; Inglis, 1984; Ward, 1991; Wells, 1994), have investigated the experiences of birth mothers who relinquished infants some years ago. Although problems of access and ethics bias many of these studies towards self-selected samples or those who are actively seeking information or help, they do provide ample evidence of the negative experiences that closed adoption practices caused for large numbers of women. They also overlap, both in the nature of the bias (towards those seeking contact) and in the model of adoption experienced (closed), with birth mothers on the Adoption Contact Register, making it reasonable to assume that many of the latter have undergone similarly distressing experiences.

Some authors consider that, without information about her child's fate, the birth mother's sense of loss is unresolvable. An early proponent of this view was Shawyer (1979), a New Zealand single mother and adoption activist, who called her book *Death by Adoption*. Within a feminist analysis, she likens the loss of a child through adoption to a bereavement, yet considers it worse than this because there is no resolution:

> Death by adoption is the death experienced by the real mother . . . It would be more bearable if the child really did die, for then she could grieve and so recover from the death. But although the child died for her, it remains very much alive for someone else.
>
> (Shawyer, 1979, p. 22)

Relinquishment has also been described as a "psychological amputation" by the American researchers, Sorosky *et al* (1984, p. 56), who conclude that birth mothers may experience deep emotional problems because social expectations of them have been entirely unrealistic. The whole experience of giving birth and placing for adoption cannot just be erased from memory. As one birth mother wrote to them: 'It's never a finished chapter, more like an open book' (p. 57). Others try to make themselves forget but find that memories can resurface. A second woman began to remember once her life with her new family was secure; her memories had been 'deep frozen and now were thawed'.

In a well-known research study, Winkler and van Keppel (1984) surveyed 213 Australian birth mothers to test whether relinquishment produced a long-lasting sense of loss. They discovered several factors affecting the degree of difficulty experienced in adjusting to the adoption, including a lack of continuing social support and of opportunity to talk about feelings: 'Every time I tried to talk I was told that it was all in the past, my life had begun again' (p. 49, quoting a birth mother). There was indeed a continuing sense of loss which, for almost half the sample of women, had intensified rather than lessened over time. The authors related it to a lack of knowledge about their child's well-being and the outcome of the placement, and to increasing hopes of a reunion as the child grew older.

In Howe's (1989) study, the 57 women who had personally visited the Post Adoption Centre in London, for individual or groupwork support over its first two-and-a-half years of operation, were sent a short questionnaire; 40 replied. Use of the Centre was highest amongst those whose adopted sons and daughters were aged around 18 and also amongst those slightly older women who, Howe thought, might have reached a stage in their personal and family lives when they were freer to attend to their own needs. (Notably, however, few had found anywhere comparable to turn to in the past so use of the Centre may reflect, too, its own recent availability to women who placed children during the peak period for adoptions in this country and who were now beginning to hear sympathetic media publicity about the needs of relinquishing mothers.) The women described thoughts and feelings which had been pent up for years, particularly of pain and guilt, and most found the Centre's services helpful; personal support and understanding and the opportunity to meet other birth mothers were both valued. The clear need 'to talk openly about the adoption of their child with a patient, sympathetic listener' (Howe, *op. cit.*, p. 30), together with the relatively high number of visits and telephone calls made to the Centre by birth mothers in counselling, reinforce the importance of offering personal support services to birth parents, including those who are considering searching and contact, since these inevitably involve unresolved feelings.

Wells (1994), herself a birth mother, born in New Zealand but now a practitioner and author in Britain, writes of the life-long trauma of the separation between mother and child after adoption. She administered questionnaires to a self-selected sample of 262 women and again found that, for just over half, thoughts about the child had increased over time; 135 thought about the child all the time or frequently (Wells, 1993b). The vast majority of those surveyed had felt under pressure and not actively involved in the decision to have the baby adopted; they later realised they had been ill-informed about what adoption involved and the alternatives to it. Virtually all now wanted basic information about their child. Progress reports while the child was growing up would have been the single most important thing that would have helped. Support and counselling over the years had also been missing. Almost all (Wells, 1993b) wanted to be found and to see their relinquished child, two-thirds had tried searching, and a majority thought they should have legal rights equal to adopted people. Interestingly, in view of current media and political interest, 'given the same circumstances today *most would decide against adoption* because of the deep and long-lasting emotional effects' (Wells, 1993b, p. 24), while the remainder would still consider adoption but only if the model employed was at least the "semi-open" one described above, accompanied by full counselling and support for the birth mother. Suggested alternatives to adoption included involving the extended family, fostering and guardianship. All of these are ways of attempting to provide a child with a warm and loving family without severing birth family ties.

Almost all the women surveyed said they had been adversely affected physically and/or mentally, and Wells (1993a) likens some of their symptoms to those of post-traumatic stress disorder. She also found a negative impact on subsequent relationships with parents, partners, children, other family and friends. Worryingly, six birth mothers who had placed within the preceding four years (Wells, 1993b, p. 25) were still describing negative emotional effects in all cases, with four having felt under pressure and three lacking counselling.

Other authors have looked quite specifically at the psychological adjustment of birth mothers. Winkler and van Keppel (1984), in the study referred to above, compared a group of 213 women in Western Australia who had relinquished babies some years before with a matched sub-sample of a representative sample. They found that the birth mothers, especially those with a strong sense of loss, had higher psychological impairment scores than the control group. Interestingly, as distinct from other forms of loss, this impact was not restricted to a specific time-period after the relinquishment. Although it is never possible to be completely certain that such a finding has not been affected by intervening events, or by other factors already present prior to the relinquishment, these researchers were satisfied by the evidence gathered overall that they had found a long-term negative impact of giving up a baby for adoption.

Field (1991) compared the emotional well-being of women with and without reunion experiences (238 with, 206 without), and considered the significance of making information available, as a result of suggestions in earlier literature that relinquishment impaired grieving and was associated with long-term guilt feelings. He analysed questionnaires returned by 444 of the 2,024 birth mothers who had sought identifying information about their relinquished children from the New Zealand Department of Social Welfare during its first two-and-a-half years of operation (see below for an explanation of New Zealand law). He found that the level of information made available to mothers about the adopted people as adults significantly influenced the mothers' psychological well-being. Lack of information was associated with significantly more intense continuing feelings of loss and guilt. Women also described feeling less powerless and uncertain after obtaining basic information about their adult sons and daughters. Those birth mothers who had experienced a reunion had typically found that nervousness and uncertainty were succeeded by joy and relief, and then by a more stable adjustment with a sense of working through feelings of loss. Field concluded that greater openness in adoption does have mental health benefits for birth mothers.

In Britain, Logan (1996a) was funded by the Mental Health Foundation to study the experiences and needs of birth parents. Twenty-eight of the birth mothers in her study were interviewed in depth; they spoke of a lack of choice about the adoption, a lack of alternatives, and a degree of coercion, often from their own mothers. The majority, even those who described satisfying lives, reported intermittent depression; 19 described themselves as having a mental health problem (for which 11 blamed the relinquishment and six were unsure), and 16 had sought treatment. A disproportionate number had been referred for specialist help, though many complained that the root cause of their problem had not been taken seriously by either GPs or psychiatrists who reportedly told women to put the adoption in the past. A sense of guilt and wanting to know what had happened to the child were particularly driving the need to search which had brought them into contact with a post-adoption service. Although the process of searching was stressful in itself, and not all contact was wholly successful, the ability to talk to staff and other birth mothers at the post-adoption service, though not sought for mental health reasons, appears often to have been of most use in gaining a different perspective. A legal right to information, as researched by Field, was not available to the British women Logan studied.

It does seem that more open adoption practice (if adoption is practised at all) may better serve the interests and needs of birth mothers. Lancette and McClure (1992), albeit in a small study, found that women involved in open adoptions who had control over the process and support throughout, although they grieved the loss of the child, appeared to feel positive about the adoption decision and not to have developed low self-esteem. Earlier studies, such as those by Iwanek (1987) and Dominick (1988), suggested, too, that contact helped adjustment to the adoption decision. Rockel and Ryburn (1988), drawing on practice experience, stated that open adoption allows birth parents to continue to be able to offer something to their child, such as knowledge of their origins, together with the information that the adoption was not a rejection. They quote a birth mother describing herself as 'back in balance' (p. 164), having developed greater confidence through being able to see her child and know who she is.

Some British authors, in asking whether the case for open adoption practice has been overstated for all parties, have questioned what we might term the "birth mother arguments", as outlined above. They have suggested that all adoptive situations involve the pain of loss (Kaniuk, 1993), and that contact would not necessarily resolve this for the birth mother since it might continually renew the grief and generate envy towards the adopters (Triseliotis, 1991, p. 26, reviewing other authors). Hughes (1996) asked a small sample of birth mothers (and two men) whether they would have wanted contact or information exchange, or thought these should be generally available. Although in favour in principle, most thought contact would have been painful in their own circumstances – perhaps because they placed their children at a time when there was insufficient choice about relinquishment. There is a tendency in all these counter-arguments to rely on speculation, however. In studies of placements where contact is *actually* taking place (see above), the conclusions are far more positive. Furthermore, and most importantly for the present study, no one has argued against information exchange or reunion when the adopted person reaches adulthood. Furthermore, if the birth mother is still experiencing loss by that point, then avoiding contact will offer no protection. On the contrary, findings such as Field's (1991), together with other work on reunion to be reviewed below, indicate that renewed contact is, in fact, both welcome and beneficial to birth mothers.

Indeed, Griffith (1991a, p. 158) points out that the erstwhile argument against opening up records to adult adopted people, that birth mothers needed protection because they wanted to 'forget about their offspring and get on with their lives in anonymity', has emerged from practice and research as a 'cruel myth'. Confidentiality, of which, in any case, no categorical assurance can ever safely be given, was not chosen by birth parents but forced on them by the law and practice of an earlier era; nor have concerns to protect birth parents, by opening the records only cautiously and partially, been raised by birth parents themselves (Griffith, 1991b, Sec.16, p. 7). For example, there had been no complaints to the Scottish Registrar General during the period when birth records were open in Scotland (since the introduction of legal adoption there in 1930) but not in England and Wales. Griffith sees openness as desirable because 'Birth mothers don't have to "live down" their past; they can now "own" their past'. Birth mothers have also emerged for the first time as real people (to quote Griffith, 1991a, p. 158), who must be fully considered in all adoption decisions.

Birth fathers

Birth fathers have been less studied than birth mothers and most of the material available is anecdotal. There are at least two book-length accounts from Canada of birth fathers' experiences (Clark, 1989; Webster, 1990) and short accounts, for example, in Wells (1994) and Feast *et al* (1994), but they are less common than the viewpoints of birth mothers. Wells, who in a book of 27 first-hand accounts includes two birth fathers, one of whom said little, and a birth grandfather, remarks that: 'if birth mothers are the silent side of the adoption triangle, then birth fathers are a mere shadow' (Wells, 1994, p. 67). They are often not even named on the birth certificate.

In the past, birth fathers were often blamed for the pregnancy and excluded from decision-making by the birth mother and/or her parents, or subjected to pressure from their own family, as well as being viewed negatively by some adoption agencies, so that they had to deal with what Wells (1994, p. 67) calls a 'double denial' – both emotional and social – of their fatherhood. There is no reason to believe that birth fathers do not have feelings of loss which may persist and intensify in the same type of circumstances as those of birth mothers, but they may have bigger cultural and sometimes legal barriers to cross in order to search for their child (if they are not named in birth or adoption records, for example). There are stereotypes of birth fathers, just as there are of birth mothers. Their circumstances range, in fact, from those who never know of their paternity or find out only years later (Clark, 1989) to those who are involved with the birth mother over many years. Even in the days of closed adoption, it was actually not uncommon for the birth mother later to marry the birth father: 23 of those in Wells', albeit self-selected, sample of women (1993b, p. 24) had done so, and as many as a third had had stable relationships with the men concerned but had faced circumstances in which they had felt unable to keep the child or had not been given the choice. This was no doubt distressing for both partners, both at the time and subsequently.

The birth father whom Wells reports at length (pp. 67–72) described having had 'stirred up feelings' in later years with which he received counselling help – in effect belatedly – to grieve the loss of the daughter he had never known. At the time of the pregnancy, he had felt out of control while the birth mother was swept along towards the adoption. Similarly, an anonymous birth father cited by Argent (1988, p. 19) describes his initial relief at being 'let off' responsibility, which was quickly displaced after the birth by an unexpected 'mixture of guilt, curiosity, the certainty of something missing' and, over time, by a crippling emotional burden resulting in a medical consultation, marriage breakdown and, more positively, later membership of a post-adoption group.

There is little research on birth fathers specifically. Often a handful, only, are present within a large sample of birth parents so that their specific views or experiences are submerged. Unusually, Deykin *et al* (1988) studied 125 birth fathers and compared the findings with an earlier study, chiefly of birth mothers. Most had thought about and a very similar proportion in each case had actually searched for the adopted person – 67 per cent of fathers and 65 per cent of mothers. Approximately half of the men had had some involvement in the adoption proceedings and most of these had approved of the decision at the time or had not opposed it; many of the others appeared to have come under pressure and still regretted the adoption. Almost three-quarters of the fathers now viewed the adoption negatively, and this was especially so for those who, typically older at the time of the birth, recalled external pressure having led to the adoption.

Birth fathers can, then, like birth mothers, experience long-term repercussions from relinquishment, including deep-seated regrets. However, in Logan's (1996) in-depth study of birth mothers, six women who subsequently married the birth father perceived their husbands as less affected by relinquishment and less involved in searching than they were themselves. The husbands' reluctance to talk about their wives' (and presumably their own) feelings and to re-open the past was acknowledged by the women concerned as being intended to protect them from distress and is, of course, stereotypically socialised male behaviour in dominant British culture. It does not, therefore, necessarily indicate an absence of care or concern at a deeper level. However, birth fathers do make far less call upon post-adoption services, including contact registers, than do birth mothers. (And men less than women more generally; Silverman *et al*, 1988, found that seven out of ten reunited birth parents who had not initiated the search had been found by daughters rather than sons.) This may be because women in most societies carry the main responsibility for the detailed work of sustaining family links. It would be useful if research could explore what practice and anecdotal accounts suggest – that some birth fathers at least *do* experience unresolved grief and a continuing need for reunion – in order to elucidate what combination of social and personal reasons holds others back from experiencing, and/or communicating, and/or acting on, these feelings. There may be others, too, who welcome reunion when it comes but who experience less motivation to pursue it themselves.

Finally, there may be factors pertaining to birth fathers which might indicate that the law or agency practice should treat them with more caution than birth mothers, and where research would be invaluable. The Deykin *et al* (1988) study cited above, for example, found that birth fathers' search activity was highly correlated with thoughts of trying to take the child back, and that the need to discover the child's whereabouts could become obsessional, whereas birth mothers searched because they felt 'a need to alleviate guilt and restore self-esteem through the assurance that the child was alive and well' (p. 248), and they had no thoughts of retrieving the child. This greater tendency towards self-interestedness (and perhaps views of fatherhood along "ownership" lines amongst fathers), as against a more child-centred approach by mothers, is not unfamiliar in relation to other contact debates (for example, post-divorce: Hester and Radford, 1996). The suggestion that those birth fathers who wanted to retrieve the child were more likely to have opposed the adoption decision implies that it may be particularly important to involve putative and legal fathers in adoption decisions but to exercise care about involving them at later stages once an adoption has taken place. (There were, however, some biases in this study in that the birth fathers concerned were involved in campaigning, a disproportionate number had married the birth mother, and more had fathered daughters than sons; any of these factors might explain the tendency to want to "reclaim" the child.)

Other relatives

There is little mention in the literature of any relatives beyond the birth parents, and certainly not in relation to researching any needs relatives may themselves have for reunion with adult adopted people. There are occasional references to fears that the lives of other family members may be disrupted if adult adopted people or birth parents trace one another. This is not generally described as a potential boon for the relatives or as something they might wish to initiate. The Department of Health Social Services Inspectorate (1995) also expresses concern that the needs of siblings might differ during childhood, so that planning continuing contact might be quite complex. It makes no comment about reunion in adulthood as it affects siblings.

In practice, however, there *are* relatives more distant than parents who are using all post-adoption services, including contact registers, and siblings appear to constitute the largest group of these. NORCAP (National Organisation for the Counselling of Adopted People) (1986) offers a small number of first-hand accounts from sisters and brothers who are delighted to have been reunited as adults. This would seem unsurprising, in fact, given the recognition in social work of the desirability of keeping siblings together in care placements (Kosonen, 1996), but there is no material on motivation for tracing siblings (for example, whether this is more likely if they have memories of one another, or have had an unhappy life and now seek compensatory experiences). Indications from practice appear to be that siblings may simply want, in adulthood, to find people to whom they are closely related. The anecdotal accounts stress physical resemblance and learning about one another's lives, for example. An attempt has been made to establish an organisation for birth siblings of adopted people – CERAFS (Council for Equal Rights under Adoption Law for Siblings). A letter from one of the founders was published in a national weekly social work journal (*Professional Social Work*, December 1994, p 8). It elicited many responses from siblings (and from social workers working with siblings) who had been unable to make contact, and had encountered great variations in post-adoption practice around Britain (see below). The letter's author, Belinda Yates, argues that siblings should be given the right to establish links as redress for the harm she believes was caused by adoption law and practice in breaking up families.

The grandparents of those who were adopted during the peak years for adoption orders might be expected to retain very mixed emotions about the placement and also now to be reaching advanced years. Only small numbers appear actively to seek contact. There is a lack of literature on their situation and views, including their reactions when contact is re-established between their child and grandchild. The Grandparents' Federation represents those who have lost contact with grandchildren through the intervention of the care system. Since practice over recent years has begun moving towards the use of adoption to provide permanent placements for children from care who, it is decided, cannot be rehabilitated, and since the Federation has experience of grandparents feeling that they have been overlooked as potential carers, there may in future years be grandparents who are actively seeking to re-establish contact with adopted children and adults. This is not yet a major focus for the organisation, however (personal communication with Noreen Tingle).

Conclusion

There is a good deal of research-based and other literature available to confirm that adoption has outgrown its "closed era", both in moral and practical terms, for a whole range of reasons. These focus particularly on the emerging needs and wishes of all parties to adoption, including the wish to do what is right for the other parties involved. Changes in outlook have, in most sections of society (though still depending on religious and cultural affiliation and political standpoint), largely ended the erstwhile view that unmarried pregnancy is shameful, that adoption provides the only real option both for unmarried mothers and their children, and that single mothers do not deserve to keep their children or have nothing to offer them.

Gone, too, are the myths that birth relatives forget the child who has been placed, that birth mothers only seek contact in order to disrupt the adoptive placement, that adopted people only search if there is something wrong with the adoption experience or with their own emotional or mental adjustment, and that adopters can only cope with a "clean break" style of placement. In all these respects we are, as a society, now more fully aware of the difficulties and the challenges inherent in the fact that 'Uniquely amongst interventions available to protect children's upbringing, adoption involves an irreversible legal separation of the child from his [sic] birth parents' (Department of Health *et al*, 1993, para. 5.2). There is a new questioning of whether and when such legal separation is desirable, and whether it need inevitably be accompanied by a complete personal and social separation.

2 The contemporary legal situation after adoption and research on its impact

Legislation, like adoption practice, has gradually moved from a "closed" model to a more open one. However, progress in this regard has been too slow to keep up with the combined impact of research findings, successful practice innovation, service user demands and international influence, not least because impending legislative change has been much delayed.

The first notable change in England and Wales came when the Children Act 1975, Section 26 (later Section 51 of the Adoption Act 1976, under consolidating legislation) gave adopted people aged 18 and over the right to apply to the Registrar General for the "linking" information which allows them to gain access to the original record of their birth. Owing to fears that this was a breach of the assurance of confidentiality given not only to adopters but particularly to birth mothers, whose lives might now be disrupted by adult adopted people reappearing on the scene, those who were adopted before 12 November 1975 are required to attend an interview with a counsellor before being given the linking information. The purpose of this meeting is 'to try and ensure that the adopted person has considered the possible effect of any enquiries both on himself and others; and that the information . . . is provided in a helpful and appropriate manner' (Department of Health and Social Security, 1976, p. 2). For those adopted after that date, counselling is optional but the person must be advised that it is available. Despite the degree of controversy, the law in England and Wales was by no means first to grant access to birth records. As mentioned above, this had been available in Scotland since the first adoption legislation was passed in 1930, and even longer in Finland, since 1926. In societies which never introduced closed adoption there were, of course, no secrets to divulge.

The emphasis in the 1975 Act on the child's best interests also had relevance to greater openness in adoption, since, amongst many other things, it implied giving consideration to maintaining contact for older children with birth family members who were significant in their lives. Child care law since that date has strengthened this emphasis on the child's interests, with the Children Act 1989 making the child's welfare 'paramount'. Adoption law is now an anomaly in that respect and the draft Adoption Bill (Department of Health and Welsh Office, 1996) states, in Clause 1(2), the intention of bringing it into line by making the child's welfare the paramount consideration of the relevant court or adoption agency – interestingly, 'in childhood *and later'* (emphasis added). This requirement to consider the child's interests as they will be in adulthood would, should the Bill be passed, be special to adoption law. It would replace the duty in the Adoption Act 1976, Section 6 (emphasis added), to give 'first consideration . . . to the need to safeguard and promote the welfare of the child *throughout his childhood'*.

One of the matters to which the court or adoption agency would be required to have regard, in determining the child's welfare, would be 'the likely effect on the child (during childhood or later) of having ceased to be a member of the original family and become an adopted person' (Clause 1[4]c). This is an explicit recognition that birth family links are significant in themselves and would have to be weighed against other factors, such as 'any harm which the child has suffered or is at risk of suffering' (Clause1[4]e). Even more so, the adoption "welfare checklist" in the draft Bill, though clearly based on the equivalent in Section 1(3) of the Children Act 1989, includes in Clause 1(4)(f) a requirement to have regard to:

> the relationship which the child has with relatives, and with any other person in relation to whom the court or agency considers the question to be relevant, including –
>
> i) the value to the child of any such relationship continuing;
> ii) the ability and willingness of any of the child's relatives, or of any such person, to provide the child with a secure environment in which the child can develop, and otherwise to meet the child's needs;
> iii) the wishes and feelings of any of the child's relatives, or of any such person, about the child.

Furthermore, the court would be under a duty to consider the whole range of its powers under the proposed Act and the Children Act 1989, and to exercise them only as necessary and as most appropriate. This could mean, for example, that a residence order under Section 8 of the Children Act, with or without a contact order or prohibited steps order (for example, explicitly to control the involvement of one or more birth relatives), might be preferred to an adoption order. Clause 86(1) would insert a new subsection (5) into Section 12 of the Children Act 1989, allowing a residence order conferring parental responsibility onto a non-parent or guardian to continue in force until the child was 18. This would clearly seem to flag up these new, longer residence orders as one legally secure (though not irreversible) alternative to adoption. As such, they might also be viewed as marking the move towards greater openness, with birth families remaining involved in children's lives, since a residence order could give parental responsibility without completely "cutting off" the past, as all now agree is wrong (Stogdon and Hall, 1993, p. 69).

In the draft Bill, the people to whom a local authority would have a *duty* to provide a service (and now a complaints procedure under clause 15) in relation to adoption would continue to extend only to the parents or guardians of persons who had been or might in future be adopted (and of course to children and adopters in actual and potential placements) and not explicitly to other birth relatives (Clause 2(1)b), although counselling and the giving of advice and information would have to be provided 'to persons in relation to adoption', rather than to any specified categories of people. As other relatives begin to voice their demands, this might begin to feel somewhat dated.

The Adoption Contact Register

Birth relatives were given their first recognition as having a need to renew contact, and adopted people their first official help with finding their relatives (as opposed to finding out who they are by obtaining birth records) when the Children Act 1989 amended the Adoption Act 1976 by adding Section 51A. This required the Registrar General to establish the Adoption Contact Register, the subject of this research study. The Register is in two parts: Part I holds the entries of "adopted persons" who wish for contact with relatives, and Part II holds the entries of "relatives". An adopted person of 18 or over who pays the fee prescribed by the Secretary of State, whose birth record is held by the Registrar General, and who has the information which would lead to a copy of his or her original birth certificate, can give notice that he or she wishes to contact "any relative" and have his or her name and address entered on Part I. It is, of course, the person's own responsibility to keep these details updated. A relative of 18 or over can be entered in Part II, on payment of a prescribed fee, in respect of an adopted person whose birth record is held by the Registrar General, on condition that he or she can prove their relationship to the person and provide the information which would lead to the original birth certificate. Section 51A(13)(a) defines "relative" for the purposes of the Register as 'any person (other than an adopted relative) who is related to the adopted person by blood (including half-blood) or marriage'. There is a slight oddness about this in that the wording reads 'is related', in the present tense, even though the parental responsibility (formerly rights and duties) of the birth parent(s) were extinguished by the making of the adoption order and the birth family is not, therefore, any longer the child's legal family. The extent to which people continue to feel personally and socially related to others from whom they have been separated for a lifetime, or whom they may never even have seen, is one of the enigmas posed again by the findings reported here. It would greatly repay further research. The Register is an important, if incomplete, recognition of this persisting feeling of "relatedness".

The legislation covers a number of matters which can be seen as safeguards for people who decide against contact or who want to pace it very carefully. Any entry in the Register can be cancelled by written notice should the person who placed it change their mind. The address given on the Register can be any address at which the person can be contacted, which means that both adopted people and relatives are free to use third parties for the receipt of any communications from the Registrar General's staff, and later from those seeking to contact them. (The use of an organisation as a third party is currently the only way in which a person registering their details can build in counselling support for themselves in the event of a link occurring with the relative(s) they are seeking.) The Register is not open to "public inspection or search" so that only those who have established their right to do so can use it to assist in seeking contact. (Indeed, it was only possible to research the Register for the present study with official permission and in a way which did not involve having any direct access to its contents.)

Those entered on Part I and Part II of the Register are treated very differently. Not only are the prescribed fees very different – currently £9.50 for adopted people and £27.50 for relatives – but the relative, though paying more, has only the right to remain on the Register and wait to be informed if there is a link with an entry on Part I. No identifying information will be sent to them. No matter who registered first, in the event of a link it is the adopted person who is sent the information held about their relative – their name and address – and who can then consider making contact, either in person or through an intermediary.

It is important to recognise in this that the adopted person is free at this point to decide that they only wanted the information, or that they have changed their mind about contact. If this happens, *the relative will hear nothing further.* He or she will know that there has been a link, and that his or her details have been passed on, but will be unable to do anything about it except wait. A person's emotional state during such a period is no doubt highly charged, even for those whose main conscious motivation for registering was to indicate openness to contact only if the other party actively wanted this. And there is perhaps bound to be a feeling of rejection if no contact comes *after* the details have been passed on, whereas hearing nothing before might only have meant that the adopted person did not know of the Register or did not feel free to use it. There was, incidentally, an odd insensitivity in the White Paper (Department of Health *et al*, 1993, Cm 2288, para. 4.22) preceding the draft Bill, in its reference to information being "exchanged" and to birth parents and adopted people being able 'to apply for the information necessary to make contact with each other', since both expressions imply a two-way channel of communication which does not exist in reality.

Interestingly, for the purposes of the study reported here, there was criticism of the form in which the Register was set up from a working party of representative organisations of all the members of the adoption triangle (Hodgkins, 1989). Although all welcomed the Register in principle, they were concerned that it lacked support, counselling, and intermediary services in connection with reunion, a letter-box service for non-identifying information, and a facility for adoptive parents to register on behalf of adopted people aged under 18. The Department of Health was understood to see the latter point as a matter for adoption agencies handling placements (and to support the facilitation of contact where desired). The opportunity to register the address of a third party was seen as an opportunity for people so wishing to obtain counselling, intermediary and letter-box services through that means. The study reported below will show whether birth relatives themselves have known about, or have considered that route to assistance to have proved adequate. One point raised by Hodgkins which remains unresolved relates to the lack of any opportunity to accompany registration with some non-disclosing information which might give the other party confidence to proceed to contact. And, although Hodgkins' brief article does refer to the need to be able to record reservations about being contacted, it certainly does not appear to have implied any wish to see a complete block on being contacted such as has now been proposed in the draft Bill (see below). Rather, there is mention of the desirability of being able to record the reason behind any reservations, together with non-disclosing information through a third party so that the enquirer, even if denied contact, would not be left with nothing. Similar non-disclosing information available in the other direction might, in any case, overcome the fears about direct contact.

A 'non contact' register

The Adoption Contact Register again features in the draft Adoption Bill, in Chapter V (Clauses 61–67), which covers registration and related matters. The biggest change over the current situation, if the Bill were to pass into law, would be, firstly, that an adopted person, instead of giving notice that he or she 'wishes to contact any relative of his' (Adoption Act 1976, Section 51A[3]), would give notice that he or she 'wishes (a) to make contact with all his relatives, or (b) to make contact only with such of his relatives as are described in the entry, or (c) not to make contact with any of his relatives'. The entry would not be made, and the fee would not be accepted, until the person had been told of any entry in

Part II showing that a relative did not wish to make contact, and the nature of the relationship. This could mean that an adopted person encountering a block on contact with their birth mother might choose not to register and could thereby lose the opportunity to contact a sister, a brother, the other parent, or any other maternal or paternal family member who might decide to register. Very careful advice would need to be given about this.

Secondly, it is proposed by the Bill that a birth relative may either give notice of wishing to contact an adopted person, as now, or, newly, that he or she does not wish to make contact (Clause 65[5]). Here again, under Clause 65(7), the relative would be informed of any wish for no contact contained in Part I before paying the fee and registering. Although this is more straightforward than for the other party, in that there is only one adopted person being sought as opposed to an unknown number of relatives, there could still be a problem if the adopted person later cancelled the negative notice and replaced it with a positive one – after counselling, say, or in the light of greater maturity, a newly developed medical condition, or any other factor. The relative who, by then, had chosen not to register, would presumably not be informed that the adopted person now wished for contact.

In the event of a link being achieved, information about any or all relatives registered, as specified by him or her, would still pass only to the adopted person and not to the birth relative. The wording in the Bill in respect of relatives is insensitive throughout in that it talks about the relative wishing to make contact, whereas the relative can only wait to *be contacted* by the adopted person – if the latter happens to be interested and aware of the Register's existence. Furthermore, although it is made clear in the Bill that all existing entries in the Register would carry over into the new system – and that they would be entered in the form of a positive wish for contact and, in the case of adopted people, as a wish for contact with all, not any specified relatives – there would doubtless, nevertheless, be much disquiet and many enquiries from people already on the Register, wondering what had happened to their entries. Only publicity could deal with this point, since it is difficult for those operating the Register to write to those entered on it without raising their hopes of a link when the letter arrives. On the other hand, it would be highly ironic if the Register were to publicise a negative change to what it offers ("no contact"), when its positive service has been so poorly publicised (see Chapter 4).

Anticipated problems with expressed wishes for "no contact" include the fact that someone encountering one could become angry or desperate and try another, less regulated search method (Post-Adoption Centre, 1990a; BAAF, 1992), which would be worrying in the light of concerns about 'the activities of some independent tracing organisations who, it was felt, did not always handle matters with appropriate sensitivity or provide the parties with adequate support' (Department of Health Social Services Inspectorate, 1995, para. 3.3v). There is practice experience in New Zealand (personal communications with professionals and activists) to suggest that people may take the stronger measure available there of vetoing the release of any information about them, not so much to prevent access to information but because of a fear of direct contact without any control mechanism. Some birth mothers there have been willing to meet their children when they have been approached sensitively, and adopted people may only want to prevent contact for a specific time period – while they have other issues in life to deal with or face opposition from adoptive parents – yet may, during that time, miss the one opportunity when the relative felt emotionally strong enough to register. Contact through an intermediary would answer the first case, and simply delaying registration (or, again, approach by an intermediary) the second. A veto is unnecessary.

There is also evidence from practice in Britain (Feast and Smith, 1993, p. 40) that adult adopted people who have not sought access to their birth records may still welcome contact when it comes because it enhances their self-esteem, sense of identity and security, and provides a bridge with the past. The agency involved in that research has altered its practice from simply leaving a birth relative's letter on file, to making contact on their behalf with the adopted person (through the adopters) because, in retrospect, adopted people had said they preferred to know someone was looking for them and to make their own minds up. It could be that some people would use a "non contact register" to block uncertainty rather than contact itself which, were it to come, they would in fact experience positively. There is evidence to support this supposition in a more recent study by Stanaway (1996/97) which found that adopted people themselves may be unaware of openness policies and initially hesitant on hearing of them. Crucially, however, when given a chance to reflect, most did want to know if a birth parent was seeking contact and many favoured intermediary involvement to ensure that they would remain in control and able to make choices should agency-mediated, birth parent-initiated contact become a possibility in their lives.

Post-adoption services

There is no detailed coverage of post-adoption services in the draft Bill. There could well be later regulation to ensure that courts and adoption agencies assess the most suitable arrangements for post-adoption contact but, nevertheless, this is a noticeable gap in the documentation published to date. Since the only real change mentioned is the essentially negative one proposing the introduction of a "non contact" register, this lack of comment on any positive policy has been taken by some to indicate a move away from the White Paper's support for increasing post-adoption contact (Department of Health *et al*, 1993, for example, paras. 4.14, 4.15 and 4.23). Indeed, at least one post-adoption service reports that some adoption agencies are reducing the degree of assistance they are prepared to give to birth relatives seeking to re-establish contact. Furthermore, regulation will arguably leave more room for continuing variation than would statute, and is also open to change by successive Secretaries of State without full consultation.

Certainly, one consequence of the current lacuna in adoption legislation and regulation in respect of post-adoption services is that adoption agency practice has developed in an 'uneven way' (Department of Health Social Services Inspectorate, 1995, p. 36), despite the 'positive and thoughtful responses' of the agencies themselves to the challenges posed by growing expectations of openness. A study of post-adoption practice in the North of England (*op. cit.*, the first SSI study of such work; 51 statutory and voluntary agencies were surveyed – 44 replied and six were visited) reveals a 'somewhat uncomfortable lack of consensus between agencies regarding the nature and extent of post-adoption services generally, and contact arrangements in particular' (p. 36). No doubt this is because they are 'at the forefront of responding to the changes that are occurring' and perhaps, one might add, because they lack up-to-date Government guidance as to what is appropriate. If agencies and their observers are 'uncomfortable', it could justifiably be asked how much more difficult it is for adopted people and birth relatives to be encountering vastly differing levels of assistance. Most agencies surveyed lacked written policies and procedures, such was the speed at which practice had had to develop. Even the terminology used had yet to settle down into an agreed usage; "contact", for example, may be direct or indirect, and may or may not involve the agency as third party (para. 1.8). There was evidence that the parties to adoption were, in some cases, moving matters on even faster than the agencies, with some adopters, for example, making their own contact arrangements (para. 2.13). Most agencies had systems for the storage and transfer of information between birth relatives and adoptive families. However, on the question of opening up previously closed placements, even to indirect contact – whether the adopted people were still children or now adult – agencies ranged from those who refused any active assistance to birth relatives seeking contact (what relatives tend to describe as encountering a 'brick wall') to those who would normally offer help, with variations of response in between – and possibly even between – individual staff members.

Almost twice as many responding agencies tended to be active than passive when the child was under 18 (64 per cent as against 36 per cent). Somewhat strangely, there was *less* activity in respect of assisting contact for relatives with over-18s (only 57 per cent, though sampled numbers are small; the difference at the extremes involves a maximum of four agencies), despite the fact that the adopted adults could not be argued to need the same level of "protection" as those who were still children. The reason was that "passive" agencies were concerned that closed placements made in an earlier era involved adopters who had not been prepared for the possibility of contact. "Active" agencies, on the other hand, considered that resourceful birth relatives would make contact anyway and that their doing so alone or through a tracing agency which did not offer support was undesirable. Thus, although twelve agencies in the SSI study said they were refusing help to relatives of adult adopted people and five were only considering it in exceptional circumstances, conversely, thirteen were offering assistance (and a further ten sometimes did) because of the extent to which they considered their highly skilled help (or that of a specialised post-adoption organisation) was needed. Even so, some of the most active were only willing to approach the adult adopted person through the adopters, and a few became active, or made a direct approach, only at and above a threshold age for the adopted person of 21 or 25. The most cautious "active" approach, taken by one very experienced agency, was to counsel birth relatives to wait until the adopted person was 25, or otherwise to approach through the adopters, on the grounds that 25 is an age of reasonable emotional maturity. Overall, once again, we read of agency 'discomfort' and a desire to receive more explicit guidance in respect of contact between adopted people and their birth relatives. This section of the SSI study report concludes:

> 'For the birth relatives and indeed for adopted children and adults, it is currently a matter of chance as to how the placing agency would react to a request from a birth parent. This seems to be far from satisfactory and suggests that this is an area requiring more detailed consideration' (para. 2.25).

The above remains the legal and practice position at the time of writing. There is nothing in the draft Bill to provide any greater clarity, even about a direction of thinking, although regulations, to be issued at a later date, may encompass this whole matter. In the meantime, some birth relatives continue to encounter what birth mothers, in particular, may well experience as a repeat of the authoritarian and punitive attitudes that marked the relinquishment itself.

An international comparison of legal rights

A useful source of overseas comparisons is a compilation by a New Zealand and international activist, Keith Griffith (1991b). What follows draws on his work (unless otherwise indicated), supplemented by contact with Australia and New Zealand for information on current legislative provision. Sachdev (1989) provides a breakdown on access to adoption and birth records in the states of the USA.

The picture is one of huge variation and of continuing change. At one extreme are Finland, where identifying information is available to adoptive parents, birth parents and adopted people at any age, and

Holland where, since 1979, adopted people have had the right to information from the age of twelve. On the other hand, several countries retain extreme secrecy; they include Russia and Japan. In the latter country, adoption is considered to be "a shameful secret" for adoptive parents and adopted children (Griffith, *op. cit.*, Section 17, p. 11).

New Zealand (see Mullender, 1991a – the main source for this subsection) is of particular relevance to the present study since, in 1985, the Adult Adoption Information Act not only followed the British example in giving adopted people access to their birth records, but also took matters a stage further by providing birth parents with the right to information – and hence the opportunity to try and trace their adopted offspring. (Legislation in England and Wales has never since caught up by rectifying its own imbalance in the rights offered.) Even so, there is not complete equity under the New Zealand legislation. Relatives other than birth parents are omitted, and a birth parent is not given information until reasonable efforts have been made to ask the adopted person whether they are willing to have their name and address revealed. There is no such safeguard in the other direction because the measure was intended for the benefit of adopted people who might not know they were adopted. A further intended safeguard which does work in both directions was introduced by the same Act in the form of an endorsement (popularly known as a "veto") on access to identifying information which can be placed by the birth parent of any person adopted before 1 March 1986, or at any date by an adopted person aged at least 19 (the age of majority being 20). A veto expires after ten years, unless renewed, or on the death of the person who placed it (although anyone who lodged their enquiry before the death occurred would not be renotified). It can be removed at the request of the person who placed it. Its effect is to block contact to any information whatsoever. Hence, an adult adopted person in New Zealand may be refused part or all of the information on their original birth certificate if the parent or parents to whom the information refers so desire(s). This cannot happen in England and Wales. (Even the "non-contact" register, proposed under the draft adoption legislation for England and Wales, would not block access to information currently available. This should be borne in mind when respondents to the research reported here, a good number of whom live overseas and have experience of the systems in force there, refer to the proposed non-contact measure as a "veto"; it might, indeed, be known as a "contact veto" in some parts of the world but there is a clear difference operationally, though not necessarily in impact, between an information veto and a contact veto.)

Vetoes have, from the start, been extremely contentious in New Zealand. Firstly, they are easily circumvented by the determined, particularly in a country with a population of under four million. And, secondly, post-adoption support groups report the distress of those who encounter them, and also consider that they encourage those placing them to remain emotionally "stuck". Only a minority have placed a veto – 6 per cent of birth mothers and 1.5 per cent of adult adopted people (Griffiths, 1997, p. 423) – and the majority of that number did so in the first year that the provision was available (*op. cit.*, pp. 427–429). These figures are further declining now that the first round of vetoes is coming up for renewal because many are not being renewed (*op. cit.*, p. 430A). Adult adopted people in a small study by Griffiths had mostly never considered a veto (*op. cit.*, p. 423). One had felt some pressure from the adopters to place one, and another had thought of using the mechanism to hurt his/her birth mother in retaliation for her perceived rejection. No one in this survey actually wanted a veto purely for themselves. Griffiths further comments that, since birth parent-initiated contact always comes through an intermediary, the adopted person already has an effective veto on letting it proceed, making the legal veto unnecessary.

On the positive side, in the first three years after the Act was passed, adopted people in New Zealand sought birth records information in a higher proportion than had been experienced in other countries, and in a ratio of more than four to one as compared to birth parents. Birth parents' reluctance to come forward seems likely to have been associated with low self-esteem (see above), with promises they had given (in that country) on oath at the time of placement, and/or with a feeling that the right to choose between privacy and searching lies more with the adopted person than with them (indicated by the fact that thousands wrote to the Department of Social Welfare to state that they were willing to welcome contact but would not initiate it). By 1991, Keith Griffith, a prominent campaigner for legislative change, was estimating that there had been 8,500 reunions in New Zealand and was reporting only six serious complaints concerning the working of the Act (in Mullender, 1991a, p. 130). Those adopted in advance of the Act are required to attend counselling before identifying information is disclosed to them, that is on the same basis as here, though the body of counsellors is more widely constituted and draws on independent adoption organisations whose staff often have personal experience of adoption. Compulsory counselling has been a contentious issue in New Zealand, but optional counselling is regarded as a valuable service. When contact is planned, either party – or the adoptive parent of an adopted child – can ask an Adult Adoption Information worker from the Department of Social Welfare to act as their intermediary. Some workers are reluctant to take on the role, however, believing that it is better for people to make the contact in a way which suits them, that delegating the experience is like "missing your own wedding" (personal communication with Adult Adoption Information worker), and that, should the approach be rejected, at least the person concerned would know they had tried their best rather than wondering whether the intermediary was to blame.

In federalised nations with separate state governments, there is variation even within that one country. In Australia, the USA and Canada, access to information varies according to the legislation of the state or province in which the adoption took place. In Canada, in addition to two provinces still offering no legal rights at all, there is a variety of registers ranging from "passive" ones with no active searching and with information only released if both parties have voluntarily registered their desire for contact, through "semi-active" ones where government social workers will search on behalf of adult adopted people only, to an active searching service for adopted people *and* birth parents (or a sibling if the birth parent is dead) by government intermediaries in British Columbia (Adoption Act 1995, Section 71). Variable fees are charged, presumably according to the amount of work involved. In the USA there is yet greater variety. Some states still have sealed records (for example, Arizona), some can be accessed by court order, some offer a voluntary register allowing adult adopted people access to identifying information, and some have an intermediary system to assist adult adopted people *and* birth parents to undertake searches (for example, Washington). In two states, there has actually been a reversal of rights: Alabama's records have been closed and, in Kansas, birth parents are 'no longer considered parties of interest' (Griffith, 1991b, Section 17, p. 2).

In Australia, where there is also a federal system, New South Wales has particularly open records with unqualified rights to identifying information for both parties (once the adopted person is 18). The state used the New Zealand system as a model but increased its degree of equity (and hence might provide a model for birth relatives' activists in the UK). On the other hand, New South Wales has a tough approach to the blocking of contact whereby, though information may be released, it is an offence to attempt contact where the party concerned has officially registered the view that this is not welcome. Most other Australian states and territories followed not the New Zealand but the Victoria state system, whereby both adult adopted people and birth relatives have a legal right to information but with official intervention. In Victoria itself, for example, an authorised agency mediates desired contact in both directions while, in Queensland, the relevant department arranges a meeting between parties when a link occurs through the state's adoption contact register, with counselling beforehand. Where counselling has been compulsory, this has been contentious; for example, in creating delays in obtaining access to the information sought and in giving professionals too much power over the situation. Most states and territories do have mechanisms to block contact, although there are grounds for seeing these as an interim measure with, for example, South Australia and Northern Territory having no veto provisions for adoption orders made under their most recent legislation. The greater involvement of intermediaries gives the parties the opportunity to consider what is involved in contact and to reconsider their views over time. A further point of interest is that there is beginning to be some consideration of the interests of non-birth family relatives of the adopted person in respect of access to information. For example, in a recent review of legislation, South Australia is considering the position of the son or daughter of a deceased adopted person who may wish to trace the adopted person's birth family background.

Research into birth parents' experience of contact and contact registers

Any reconsideration of the legal rights currently afforded to birth relatives needs to be informed by research. There have been a number of studies of birth parents' attitudes towards, and experience of, searching, contact and reunion with adopted people in adulthood.

In the USA, Sorosky *et al* (1984) carried out a small-scale follow-up study of 36 female and two male birth parents. Most had placed 10 to 33 years previously; all had placed infants. Half still felt loss, pain and mourning, while 82 per cent wondered various things about the adopted person now, and the same percentage would have been amenable to a reunion with the adult adopted person. Eighty-seven per cent stressed that they did not wish to hurt the adoptive parents; none was looking for a parental relationship. Four out of five agreed with the idea of making intermediaries available to assist the emotionally difficult reunion process. Ninety-five per cent were interested in updating the information about themselves on agency files so as to give enquiring adopted people a truer impression of their current circumstances.

Also in the USA, Silverman *et al* (1988, cited by Griffith, 1991b, Section 5, pp. 6–7) studied 170 reunited birth parents, 79 per cent of whom initiated their own searches and 21 per cent of whom were found by their children. The birth parents had experienced traditional closed adoptions, often made under some pressure, and 94 per cent had experienced grief more severe than anticipated, which mainly had not lessened over time. Motivations to search had included media coverage and greater social acceptance. Most had had support: 63 per cent from a peer support group, 11 per cent from an adoption agency, and 10 per cent from a mental health professional, but most did not use an agency intermediary – perhaps because they wanted to take the control over the process that they had lacked at the time of relinquishment. Over 80 per cent wrote or telephoned as the first means of contact. Of the whole sample, 60 per cent felt very positive about contact and only eight per cent experienced rejection; 98 per cent of those who had achieved reunion would have had it no other way. There were clear benefits in self-esteem, a release of energy, a healing effect, and knowing their child was well and knew in turn that he or she was wanted and cared about. Reunions were not experienced as disruptive of current lives and, importantly in relation to proposed blocks on contact, even those who had not searched and still would not do so were often pleased after they had been traced.

Howe (1989) surveyed birth parents who were in touch with the Post-Adoption Centre in London. Of 1,246 birth parents who had contacted or been referred to the Centre, 96 per cent were birth mothers. Of these, just over 60 per cent wished to search for or find out about the adopted child, and almost a quarter needed personal counselling over the loss of their child. One of the peak times for use of the Centre was when the adopted person would be reaching young adulthood, perhaps because the birth mothers knew of adopted people's right to obtain birth records information at 18 or over.

Sachdev (1989) was critical of earlier studies as largely anecdotal or based on small, biased samples, often drawn from clinical or activist populations or recruited through the media. His own random sample involved all sides of what might be termed the adoption "rectangle" (i.e. including adoption workers), but lacked birth fathers and other birth relatives besides mothers. Using the records of the Eastern Canadian Department of Social Welfare, he interviewed 300 people, 78 of whom were birth mothers divided evenly between a sub-group who relinquished in 1968 and the rest in 1978. It was hoped to compare attitudes over time towards opening up sealed adoption records, but earlier files gave too little information to locate the women concerned. Birth mothers strongly supported providing adult adopted people with identifying information (younger birth mothers more strongly than older ones), and non-identifying information at any age. Half of the birth mothers would have been happy to have provided periodically updated medical information. All adoption triangle respondents (adopted people, adoptive parents, birth mothers) overwhelmingly supported the release to birth mothers, on request, of non-identifying information throughout the adopted person's childhood. Seven out of ten birth mothers supported disclosure of adult adopted people's whereabouts to birth mothers, around half to birth fathers, and two-thirds to birth siblings. All triangle sub-samples strongly supported widely publicised contact registers with active searches to locate birth mothers, although birth mothers themselves did not feel they had the right to claim equity in this regard. Majorities of all groups supported the department acting as intermediary and arranging the first meeting. Thus a random study again backed post-adoption contact, as biased samples had done.

An earlier Canadian study by Garber (1985, cited in Griffith, 1991b, Section 5, p. 5), gave more detail on the difference in response to reunion according to the age of the birth mother. Those who were 60 and over were less eager to have their past revealed but, if they were to learn that their child needed to know about his or her own past, said they would want to be helpful. Those in their 40s and 50s saw the value of contact and had fewer reservations about their past pregnancy being revealed. Younger birth mothers were still angry about having had to relinquish their child and were looking forward to reunion. There could well be a link here with changing social attitudes. The older mothers placed their children at a time when guilt and shame predominated, whereas the youngest mothers may have been most affected by the shift towards beginning to see birth mothers as having rights and closed adoptions as often undesirable (and perhaps by contested adoptions).

A publication from the Post-Adoption Centre (1990b) in England outlines themes raised by birth mothers meeting there in groups. These included: feelings of loss; guilt and anger at society's attitudes towards them; the need for, at least, non-identifying information, together with being informed if the adopted person died; the right to trace – 'Some mothers feel the process of tracing is almost a recipe for survival' (p. 4); dilemmas around their "rights"; and greater openness and information exchange in adoption in the future. Some feared that a reunion would reveal differences in class, attitude and expectations; this would be compounded by the barriers inherent in a transracial placement and black mothers also feared that the child might have encountered racism or the denial of their black identity while growing up. This might indicate the need for support and counselling services able to encompass these additional issues. A discussion day held at the Post-Adoption Centre in 1988 (Fitsell, 1989) also produced feedback from small group discussion and included a call for a contact register with equal rights for adopted people and birth mothers, and many other services such as information exchange and counselling.

Field's (1991) study of birth mothers contacting the New Zealand

Department of Social Welfare considered the significance of the availability of information and of reunions, particularly their impact on women's emotional health (see above). He found that women often delayed searching due to anxiety as to whether the adopted person knew he or she was adopted, whether the birth parent would be considered a threat by the adoptive parents, and because the birth parent had to overcome her own reduced self-esteem – a result of the long-term stigma of birth outside marriage and of socially induced guilt about giving up the baby. Birth mothers in this study were noticeably more stable emotionally following an initial reunion, and even discovering basic information reduced feelings of powerlessness. A majority were satisfied with the renewed contact, the chief remaining wish being for greater closeness, sometimes geographically. Almost half had lacked counselling prior to reunion (which others had found helped significantly in preparing for the experience), and three-quarters lacked counselling afterwards. Such support might have assisted those who felt some disappointment with the relationship achieved, or who were upset by feelings evoked by the initial reunion, to be prepared for these eventualities although it cannot, as Field's respondents reported, prevent them. A small group of 21 women who were interviewed in depth were evenly split on whether the minimum age of 20 for adopted people to access information should be lowered, and on the question of vetoes. In addition, some thought there should be greater equity between their own rights and those of the adopted person. The difficulty of 'balancing rights of privacy and rights to know' (p. 151) was clear. Field concludes that his findings confirm 'the mental health benefits of more recent open adoption practices in New Zealand and elsewhere' (*loc. cit.*) and that a majority of birth mothers who do achieve contact are satisfied.

Reunions in practice

In-depth interviews with 30 birth mothers by Gediman and Brown (1989, cited by Griffith, 1991b, Section 5, pp. 9–10) revealed that the hard work of reunion begins after the initial meeting: filling gaps in information; sensitively handling difficult information on both sides (such as unhappy adoption experiences, or facts about paternity or the circumstances of conception); coming to terms with the past; informing and dealing with the current families of both parties; and, most importantly, negotiating a mutually acceptable relationship despite differences in values or lifestyles. Notwithstanding the problems that some encountered, such as sexual attraction or emotional disturbance, most birth mothers interviewed considered reunion to be successful because they and the adopted person were now part of each other's lives. Most also felt a sense of healing taking place. The Post-Adoption Centre (1990a) held a consultation day involving 34 people, including nine birth relatives. A questionnaire exercise revealed that engaging current partners in the process and explaining matters to subsequent children were amongst the key issues for birth mothers. A counsellor was seen as potentially helpful.

A handbook on preparing for reunion is available (Feast *et al*, 1994), with advice addressed largely to adopted people and personal accounts by all parties, including adoptive parents. In fact, many of the topics covered in the opening chapter are equally relevant to birth parents. There is considerable emphasis on fears of rejection, with assistance to understand that a refusal of contact may relate to the other person's circumstances, feelings, need to protect others, or, perhaps, painful memories, rather than to the searcher personally. There is evidence from these first-hand accounts that relatives may place their name on a contact register, and follow through to reunion, out of consideration for the adopted person's needs as well as their own. For example, one birth mother, as well as wanting information and reassurance for herself, commented: 'I felt it wasn't "fair" not to write to him. I thought it would be like another rejection, if he felt that his adoption had already been one rejection.' As with open placements, then, it seems that research studies and practice accounts based on situations where openness (here, reunion) has actually happened have positive messages. A further point in common is that both show birth mothers as not only able but anxious to put their children's interests before their own.

Research on contact registers

There are few scholarly accounts of contact registers in operation. The two papers reported here both stem from the same research team in Scotland.

Focusing primarily on the adopted adults' experience, Lambert *et al* (1992) compared the Registrar General's Adoption Contact Register in England and Wales with the Birthlink register in Scotland. The latter, they considered, offers 'a more personal service to both parties' (as opposed to simply sending the name and address of the relative to the adopted person in the event of a link), since it includes in-built counselling by the parent agency's adoption counsellors. The counsellor helps both parties to consider how best to move towards reunion, and identifying information is not exchanged until both feel ready. The application form for Birthlink also provides space in which a birth parent who does not wish for contact can explain the reasons behind this decision and pass on some information about him- or herself. This personal information, including something about why the adoption occurred, is equally useful in facilitating the process of reunion where it does occur. The authors comment on the fact that searchers utilising other methods frequently need advice and support, with a particular tendency for adopted people to have sought professional help either when things became difficult or when preparing for a reunion. Lambert *et al* regard contact registers as useful but passive and haphazard, since all they can do is signal 'a willingness to be contacted if this is also desired by the other party'. There is no result unless both parties hear about the register and both take the step of registering – which makes publicity important. Birthlink distributed leaflets about its service through voluntary agencies and social work departments and made active use of the media to disseminate information. Adopted people applying for access to birth records are informed through leaflets about the relevant register, both in Scotland and in England and Wales, but there is no equivalent way of reaching birth relatives, amongst whom, those involved with placements made many years previously may never have heard of the register service or that the law has changed in their favour, at least a little, in England and Wales.

In a small-scale but detailed study, Bouchier *et al* (1991) interviewed 46 Scottish birth mothers (some of adult, others of younger adopted people, relinquished at least eight years before), following the setting up of Birthlink. Five of the women were opposed to contact (though three would have liked information) and the rest were eager for contact. Of the latter group, 85 per cent thought about their child weekly or even daily, and over a third of the whole group interviewed felt they had adjusted only poorly or not at all to the relinquishment experience. Almost all considered that personal relationships with one or more of their family members had been adversely affected. Those who had lacked family or professional support in the year after placement, and those who thought frequently about the child, appeared to have poorer emotional and physical health than the rest.

Two-thirds of those seeking contact thought birth mothers should have the same right to information as adopted people. Some mentioned building safeguards into the system if this were to happen, and several thought the threshold age of the adopted person should be higher in the case of a birth mother seeking information at, for example, 21 (as opposed to 17 for adopted people accessing their birth records in Scotland). Almost all the birth mothers seeking information felt that it would help them with current feelings and some said it would also prepare other family members in case the adopted person made contact. Just under two-thirds planned to use an intermediary. Eighty per cent wanted to meet the adopters as well as the adopted person, often to thank them and to reassure them that they had no intention of disrupting the adoptive relationship.

Of those opposed to contact, four out of five still favoured leaving information with the Birthlink register for the adopted person, in some cases with a note explaining why they did not want to be contacted. Four out of the five would have reconsidered contact if they had learnt that the adopted person really needed it, and several appeared to have reached their decision to oppose contact chiefly because of other family members. These matters are of relevance in relation to any "non-contact" provision which may be considered for England and Wales, even though the number in this sub-sample was so small.

Most of the mothers in the Bouchier *et al* study drew a distinction between transferring parental rights to adoptive parents and denying information to birth mothers. They refused to believe that the legislation intended the latter and, certainly, it need not logically follow; some considered that significant events in the child's life, particularly death, but also any breakdown in the adoptive family or other reason why the child might need help, should be communicated immediately to birth parents. A commonly expressed suggestion was for regularly updated, non-disclosing progress reports to be made to the agency by both the adoptive and birth families, to satisfy the information needs of the other party. For example, the birth mother's need to know that the child was well and thriving and, when he or she reached adulthood, whether contact was being contemplated. The authors comment: 'An effective method of exchanging information emerged as the most fundamental and valuable improvement to post-adoption support services suggested by the relinquishing mothers who participated in this study.' For the future, adoption agencies seemed the natural bodies to perform the service of holding regularly updated information and, where necessary, reminding parties to supply it. This amounts to continuing indirect contact through a third party. The current lack of reciprocal rights, even to non-disclosing information, was equated with the punitive attitudes birth mothers experienced in the past, when many reported having no control over and no real choice in what happened. There is an enormous amount in this research study which needs to continue influencing improvements both in adoption placement practice and post-adoption work throughout childhood, but it also has much to say about birth mothers' continuing needs for information and, often, reunion. The authors conclude that Britain has yet to engage fully with the rights of all the individuals involved in adoption (pp. 106–107).

Conclusion

Current placement policy continues to open up and information exchange (see Logan, 1996b for an evaluation of one such scheme) is increasingly offered by adoption agencies to birth relatives and adopted people still in childhood. It is post-adoption practice as it concerns adult adopted people which is marked by the greatest variation in agency approach and hence in the responses birth relatives receive from adoption workers. These continue to range from what is experienced as a "brick wall" refusal to help re-initiate contact, to the most sensitive and active intervention on relatives' behalf, with help in tracing accompanied by voluntary counselling and intermediary services. It is in the midst of this variation that adoption contact registers operate.

Relatives themselves repeatedly express a strong need for information about, and often contact with, adopted people who have now reached adulthood, and many consider that this should be their right. Those who hold back from pursuing contact, like the adopted people studied by Haimes and Timms, do so because they are thinking of others. Adopted adults, according to Haimes and Timms, frequently fear upsetting their adoptive parents. Most birth mothers who placed infants have an equivalent fear of disrupting the lives of their adopted offspring, in the interests of whose stability, after all, the relinquishment occurred. Nevertheless, the awkward balance to be struck between rights to search and rights to privacy, together with the modern practice of placing the children of those we might term more "difficult" parents (as opposed to parents in difficulties), evokes the question of possible safeguards such as, for example, the use of intermediaries and the proposal to introduce "non-contact" registrations, though these can be as contentious as the problems they are intended to resolve. The legacy of relinquishment and the experience of those who have had reunions suggest, too, that the provision of counselling services should be fully considered in any context related to renewed contact, though even counselling has become controversial where it has been imposed as an authoritarian form of protection or a political compromise. Consequently, it is important that personal support remains voluntary.

Although the service offered by the Adoption Contact Register is enshrined in statute, and is therefore currently clear cut, it is nevertheless located within a field – that of post-adoption contact – which is subject to rapid change, potentially conflicting interests and increasingly vocal demands. Its own scope is bound to be exposed to question as a result.

The Register is called upon in Part II to serve a group in which every individual has been personally affected by the most extreme form of adoption, the "closed" and secretive model which we can now recognise as a form of social engineering that took too little account of people's emotional and social needs. Since social and professional attitudes have swung away from considering the closed model acceptable (other than in exceptional circumstances), this is an appropriate time to ask birth relatives whose names are on the Register the extent to which it meets their needs or whether it, too, should become involved in a process of careful change. Although the Register serves two constituencies of users, it provides only a one-way information channel and, as such, it has been overtaken by probably a majority of adoption agencies, assuming that the SSI study (Department of Health Social Services Inspectorate, 1995) is generalisable. This, too, makes posing the question of change unavoidable.

Since there is more than one generation of relatives registering (for example, brothers and sisters as well as birth parents of younger adults), and since some closed (or only semi-open) placements are still being made, the Register will continue to be needed for some time. In the future, it is likely that the views of birth relatives will be heard more loudly in our society than hitherto. This will involve a greater complexity than much of the literature to date reflects, in that it is beginning to emerge that birth fathers and siblings may take different stances from birth mothers. It is likely, too, that overall progress towards greater openness in adoption will be undiminished. Certainly, discussion in this country has moved from debating the principle of openness, to determining the extent of its applicability in the prevailing national context and the best ways to manage it. It is important to plan ahead, particularly while the whole question of adoption law reform is under active review, and to consider what official line is to be taken about the needs and demands of birth relatives to re-enter the lives of adult adopted people. The chapters which follow, and which relate the detailed findings of the research study, will cast some light upon what birth relatives think of the statutory line taken so far and what they would ideally like to see in its place.

3 Methodology of the research

Background

The project involved seeking the views of people whose details were placed on Part II of the Adoption Contact Register, as administered in Southport, Merseyside (under the aegis of the Registrar General) by the Adoptions Section of the then Office of Population Censuses and Surveys (OPCS), which became part of the Office for National Statistics (ONS) on 1 April 1996. This body will normally be referred to as "ONS" throughout this book, so that the text does not immediately assume a dated air, even though the organisation was still called OPCS during the period when the data was collected (and was so known to participants in the research). It is hoped that this decision will not give rise to too much confusion in the dissemination of the research findings.

The objectives of the study were:

- to measure the use of the Adoption Contact Register by birth relatives of adopted people: who uses it, why, and with what results;
- to test the hypothesis that, for those relatives using the Register, it still has not given them the extent of legal rights that many would like but that it may not be easy for birth relatives to exercise even their current rights because they fear encroaching on the adopted person's life and because of their own emotional "baggage";
- to identify the experiences, aspirations, concerns and wider needs of birth parents who contact the Register;
- to ascertain their views on the proposed right to express a wish not to be contacted; and
- to look for any notable trends in Register use by birth relatives: for example, male versus female use; use by different categories of relatives; any factors "triggering" use of the Register, as against a generalised "need to know"; use of the Register as against use of other services.

Some further objectives which might have been considered were not pursued because the research had to stay focused. These included mental health issues affecting respondents.

In the longer term, it was hoped:

- to explore the social policy implications of changing attitudes experienced by birth parents who have lost a child to "closed" adoption, and of birth relatives' own changing attitudes (for example, towards the "right", or otherwise, to re-enter the adopted person's life); and
- to make recommendations for future law and policy development in the post-adoption field at a time when this is under active review.

The sample

Part II of the Adoption Contact Register is reserved for those related to adopted adults by blood or by marriage. Potentially, the project had access to everyone whose details had been entered in that part of the Register between the starting-date of the Register's operation, 1 May 1991, and the cut-off date of 30 September 1995, chosen by the researchers as the baseline date. The number of people registered in Part II at that point was 3,404.

Of this potential number, 69 per cent (2,346) agreed to participate in the survey and, subsequently, 76 per cent of these returned the completed questionnaire (1,784 people, or 52 per cent of the potential total). This was a remarkably good response rate for a postal questionnaire and a measure of the importance to respondents of having their views sought. It had been predicted by those members of the project advisory group who were involved in post-adoption work, in the light of the invisibility of birth relatives of adopted people hitherto and their lack of a voice, that respondents would be keen to participate and that many would write copiously on the questionnaires. Both predictions were proved correct. The length of the questionnaire – which exceeded textbook recommendations (such was the temptation to seize this rare opportunity of obtaining the views of birth relatives) – proved not to be a disincentive, despite the warnings of seasoned researchers. In the event, the topic of adoption proved to be a special case because relatives had been silenced in the past and took the opportunity to break that silence. This bears out Field's (1991) finding that once birth relatives (in his case birth mothers) have consented to participate, even though they have not at that stage seen the size or contents of the questionnaire, a high proportion of them will actually do so because they feel strongly about finally having an opportunity to share their views and experiences on losing a relative through closed adoption. Field had 444 usable questionnaires from 551 participation consents; 81 per cent compared with 76 per cent in the present study. It is notable, however, that out of a population of 2,024 birth mothers (those who had sought identifying information in New Zealand during the qualifying period for his research sample), the 444 returned questionnaires represented a self-selected sample of 22 per cent (and 27 per cent agreed but did not all comply), as compared with 52 per cent self-selected respondents and 69 per cent consents in the present study. In other words, the present sample, though skewed in three ways – in being on the Register, in agreeing to be in the sample and in returning the questionnaire – is numerically more representative of the population sampled than Field's.

A total of 562 people who had agreed to participate in the present study did not return questionnaires or, in eight cases, returned them too late to be included in the analysis of responses. There were also three written refusals to participate after people had seen the questionnaire, one questionnaire returned blank by the spouse of a deceased person on the Register (who had now realised he could not answer the questions in her stead), and one returned blank from an out-of-date contact address. Also, duplicate forms were returned by one birth relative who was on the Register in respect of adopted twins, only one of which was analysed since the views of only one respondent were involved. Because of an awareness that some non-respondents would have been more upset by reading the questionnaire than they had anticipated, so that the last thing they might want would be another letter from the researchers, it was decided, following discussion with the Advisory Group, not to send a reminder letter to pursue non-returned questionnaires. Further reasons for making this decision were the high return rate – at 76 per cent of these agreeing – and the sheer volume of work.

Even had the response rate been raised above 76 per cent, this would not have made the sample more representative in terms of the numerically larger missing group – the half or so of those on the Register who did not wish to participate – nor in relation to birth relatives as a whole in the population. In other words, this was always bound to be a skewed sample and it achieved a reasonable degree of representativeness within its own terms. It is impossible to know what detailed effect the inevitable biases have upon the sample. The population on the Register, by definition, consists of those who are willing to be contacted by the adopted person, and probably mainly those who would actively welcome contact. It is acknowledged that there could be other birth relatives who would oppose contact and whose views it will not be possible to represent here. Nevertheless, since a major aim of the project was to comment on the operation of Part II of the Register itself, surveying its own users was the most logical thing to do. Furthermore, since it is extremely difficult to access any sample of birth relatives affected by closed adoption, such is the secrecy and distress surrounding the whole issue, the opportunity of asking wider questions about adoption more generally was not to be undervalued. The biased nature of our sample is readily acknowledged, but the sheer number of responses still makes the data useful, for example, in relation to the process of adoption law review and to obtaining the views of some groups of relatives, notably siblings, who have rarely featured in other work.

It is possible to offer some idea, though less than would ideally be liked, of the degree of representativeness of the self-selected sample as against the total population of those relatives who had registered by the cut-off date. Here, the researchers were reliant on the demographic detail collected and recorded on computer at the point of entering details upon the Register. Further information, such as the age of those registered (since the ages of the sample are known), could have been gleaned by asking ONS staff to undertake a manual check of the records (birth certificates would carry further information), but it was not considered that this painstaking work with 1,784 files (or the expense involved) was justified.

The 3,404 on the Register included 429 males (12.6 per cent) and 2,974 females (87.4 per cent) with one not known. The 1,784 in the sample included 203 males (11.4 per cent) and 1,571 females (88 per cent), with 10 not known because the relevant question was not answered. These are remarkably similar proportions so there is little risk of gender bias in the responses as against the Register.

Figure 1
Respondents by gender

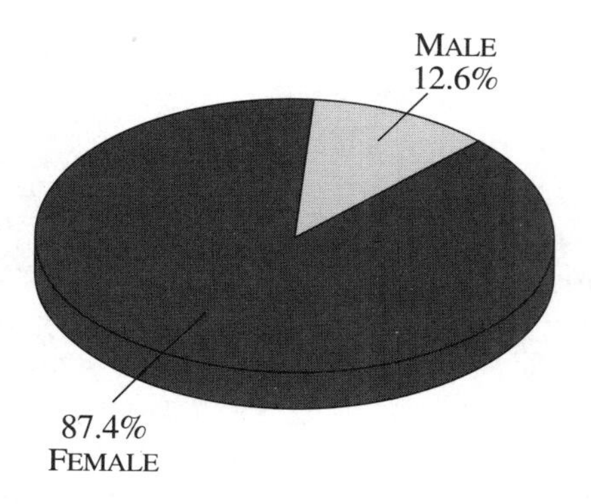

The relationship to the adopted person of those on the Register and in the sample was as follows:

Table 1
Degree of relationship to the adopted person

Relationship	No. on Register	%	No. in sample	%
Mother	2,382	79.1	1,276	71.9
Father	157	5.2	68	3.8
Sibling	296	9.8	347	19.6
Grandparent	68	2.3	32	1.8
Aunt/uncle	71	2.4	33	1.9
Other relative	36	1.2	18	1.0
Total	3,010	100.0	1,774	100.0
Missing cases	394		10	

There are some differences in the way the above information has been recorded by the Office of National Statistics in relation to the Register and by the current study, which make an exact comparison difficult. It was not possible to build in a more precise coincidence of categories because the ONS data were not available in time to influence the design of the questionnaire. There is no equivalent in the study sample for the looser ONS categories of half- and step-relation so these have been treated as missing cases and the percentages calculated without them. (Many are thought to be half-siblings, however, which would explain why there appear to be more siblings in the sample than on the Register! If all the ONS missing cases were siblings, the percentage of siblings on the Register would rise to 20.3%.) The missing cases in the survey data are non-responses. As will be apparent, birth mothers are a little under-represented in the study and siblings are very well represented. Previous literature has provided at least the beginning of some information about birth mothers but next to nothing about siblings, so it is interesting to have so many here. This has given rise to the idea of undertaking further, in-depth work with them, which is currently in train. Chapter 9 is devoted largely to sibling-related issues arising from the main research study.

It is impossible to say whether the study was representative in terms of age, since Register information was not available, but some other comments about age groups are possible. The sample had more respondents in their middle years than older or younger. There were 253 aged under 40 (including only 41 aged under 30), 239 aged 60 and over, and the bulk in between, with 718 in their 40s and 562 in their 50s. This coincides with Howe's (1989) finding about birth mothers that they tended to use post-adoption services when their adopted children reached adulthood and when they themselves were in their middle years, with perhaps fewer family responsibilities and concerns (for example, actual or potential views of other family members) preventing them from pursuing a matter of great personal concern to themselves. The study sample also include some considerably older mothers and older siblings, who, in some cases (according to the questionnaires) wanted to try and find the adopted person before they died.

Although ages are not available for the Register (Part II) as a whole, there is information as to the year of birth (and hence ages) of the adopted people in respect of whom relatives have registered. Taking their ages as at 31 December 1995, the oldest was 85 and the youngest was one year of age. There were 66 adopted people of 60 and over being sought and, interestingly, nine of these were born before the first adoption act was passed in this country; they may, of course, have been placed in infancy and adopted later. The bulk of adopted people being sought are young adults.

Table 2

Ages of adopted people in respect of whom relatives have registered and of relatives in study

Age	Of adoptee sought (all Part II)	Of relative in sample
<17	97	0
18–19	86	0
20–29	1,403	41
30–39	1,129	212
40–49	425	718
50–59	198	562
60<	66	239
Total	3,404	1,772
Missing cases	0	12

Putting the two tables together (and always remembering that there are approximately twice as many people in the first column as in the second because the former represents the adopted people in respect of whom everyone on Part II has registered, while the latter only includes those relatives in the sample) shows the pattern of a predominance of mothers in their middle years searching for adopted people whose births coincided with the peak years for baby adoption. The Register peaks at births in 1966–68, with relatives seeking 200, 216 and 208 people born respectively in those years. No other years exceed 200. There is a gradual rise to that peak, but the availability of abortion and contraception in the late 1960s, together with changing attitudes towards lone mothers, have caused a much steeper drop away from it, for example, only 116 adopted people born in 1969. Ninety-seven of those with whom contact is welcome or desired are, as yet, too young to go onto Part I of the Register – the youngest only one or two years old at the time of writing. This would suggest that some closed adoptions are continuing to be made, perhaps in contested proceedings, or at least that some relatives are being excluded from contact. There are 94 people in the sample whose adopted relatives were the subject of contested adoptions, the low number probably reflecting the early date of many of the adoptions concerned. This may become a numerically significant reason for registration in future years since adoption has come to be used more frequently to place children from care whose birth parents not untypically oppose the measure. On the other hand, these placements may involve far more information exchange than in the past, which may make contact through this route less necessary.

There is no information available about the ethnic origin of relatives on the Register. Of those in the study sample, 98.9 per cent described themselves as white, as against 94.5 per cent in the population of Great Britain as at the 1991 Census (slightly lower in England and Wales alone). All African-Caribbean and Asian ethnic groups are under-represented in the sample, with only 19 individuals overall describing themselves in any category other than white (including those of mixed parentage). They include, for example, four African-Caribbean and three Chinese relatives. Slightly more people (34) stated that the adopted person with whom they would welcome contact had been adopted transracially, which suggests either that some black people did not answer the ethnic origin question (there were 37 non-responses) or that there was confusion for a few people as to the meaning of a transracial placement (which the questionnaire admittedly did not explain). There is no way of knowing whether this number is proportionate to the transracially adopted population as a whole or to that reflected in either Part I or Part II of the Register but, certainly, the early date of many of the adoptions concerned would pre-date the years when transracial placements were at their height. The low level of publicity given to the Register (see Findings), and the failure to publicise or explain it in any language other than English, is likely to disadvantage members of minority ethnic communities disproportionately. If any renewed publicity is planned in the future, it should pay attention not only to the language issue, but also to where posters, leaflets and other materials are placed; community centres, places of worship, women's groups, and so on across all communities should be asked to carry information.

There is no information available about the educational qualifications or employment status of relatives on the Register as a whole. The study sample included more people with professional and higher educational qualifications than the general population of Great Britain, and a much lower proportion of people without any formal qualifications (17.4 per cent as against 28 per cent). It shows 64 per cent economically active, across a not untypical spread of occupational classifications given the gender bias in the sample. The overall educational bias may indicate that a good number of those birth mothers who placed their babies for adoption in order to complete their own education were able to do so successfully. The large number of relatives in the sample with professional qualifications may also coincide with a greater opportunity for professional people to have seen the publicity for the Register, or to have heard it mentioned by word of mouth, in public buildings or in relation to health and welfare services of various kinds, for example. Importantly, too, there is likely to be a bias in the Register towards those who can afford the fee, and in the sample towards those who could most easily cope with lengthy documents and with expressing their thoughts in written form. Hence, the lower socio-economic groups may be under-represented. It is reasonable to assume that the under-represented groups have equally strong views, but no way of knowing whether these would differ in substance.

One interesting feature which emerged from the research, both in relation to those relatives who had registered their details and those who participated in the research, was the number who lived overseas. Of the 3,404 on the Register at 30 September 1995, 486 were resident overseas (14 per cent). Of those who returned questionnaires, 314 lived overseas (18 per cent), making overseas respondents slightly over-represented (having constituted 16 per cent of those who agreed to participate, they were proportionately better at returning their forms). The main point of interest here is the high number of overseas residents who are using the Register. The most likely reason would appear to be the greater prominence given to relatives' rights in some other countries, such as New Zealand and parts of Australia, the USA and Canada – the countries, in fact, where the largest groups of overseas respondents in the sample were living. This supposition about publicity assisting participation in the survey is borne out by detailed comments on questionnaires revealing the anger some overseas residents had felt when they first discovered that their rights were far fewer than those of their compatriots because the information they sought was held in England and Wales. Other reasons for the high number of overseas residents on the Register as a whole might include birth mothers going overseas to "start a new life" following a relinquishment for adoption, but there is no way of checking this.

The number of overseas residents, and the range of countries in which they were living (literally all over the world) led to some quite complicated work by the project's Research Assistant in discovering how to pre-pay the return by post of heavy questionnaires in large envelopes (the norm to which the Royal Mail works being a single folded sheet of paper). Her persistence eventually bore fruit, however, and none of the non-returns was caused by postal difficulties, so far as the researchers are aware.

In terms of region of residence within Britain, a comparison has been made between those in the sample and those on Part II of the Register as a whole. It was not possible to be precise since the information was not collected in exactly the same ways. Questionnaire respondents were asked to tick a list of alternatives (as in the table below) which may have resulted in some blurring between, for example, the "North" and the "North West". The assembling of data for the Register as a whole was difficult because no information is held in anything like this form and, of course, it was crucially important not to breach confidentiality in relation to whereabouts. The researchers requested a listing of just the first two letters of relatives' postcodes (as a simple frequency list, with absolutely no further information so that confidentiality was not breached) and assembled these by region, with some help from the Royal Mail for the more obscure ones. This was the only data from ONS for which there were genuinely missing cases and, in fact, it has only been possible to calculate percentages from a list of 2,632 postcodes (first two letters) not the full 3,404 on Part II of the Register. However, the closeness of fit between percentages in the sample and those amongst the 2,632 postcodes suggests that this has not caused too much misrepresentation. What emerges is, in fact, a reasonable degree of representativeness of the sample as against the Register. Table 3 shows the two sets of figures and percentages for the Register Part II and the sample.

Table 3
Region of residence in England and Wales

Region	Register Part II (n)	%	Sample (n)	%
North	85	3.3	50	4.1
North West	367	14.1	156	12.8
Yorks/Humberside	264	10.2	91	7.5
Midlands	361	13.9	189	15.5
Wales	35	1.3	21	1.7
East Anglia	148	5.7	70	5.7
South West	326	12.6	152	12.5
South East	1,008	38.9	490	40.2
Total	2,594	100.0	1,548	100.0
Missing cases	810		200	

As can be seen from the table, the sample, as against the Register, slightly under-represents the North West and Yorkshire and Humberside, and slightly over-represents the North, the Midlands, Wales, and the South East. The differences are mainly small and the other two regions are almost precisely represented. No reason can be suggested for the variations, although there was agency involvement in the Advisory Group from both the North and the Midlands so it is possible that more respondents there knew the study was going on or had faith in it. On a rough comparison with national population data (not shown) the Register itself strikingly under-represents the population of Wales. This is thought, both by ONS staff and by post-adoption practitioners in Wales, to reflect the lower number of adoption orders made there. It is also worth raising the point that the Register has never been publicised, and that those administering it do not supply documentation in any language other than English, so Welsh speakers, like members of other minority ethnic groups in Britain, could be disadvantaged in learning of its applicability to them. A small number of those using the Register not shown are now resident in Scotland, although they are desirous of contact with adopted people whose records are held in England.

One other comparison is possible between the sample and the Register as a whole. The number of matches achieved by respondents to the research (72) can be compared with the number achieved by registered people overall (108) at the date set as the cut-off for inclusion in the study. This demonstrates that precisely two-thirds (66.66 per cent) of the "linked" relatives are in the self-selected sample of respondents, whereas the overall participation rate was 52 per cent. In other words, a greater proportion of the "linked" than of the "unlinked" relatives features in the responses reported below. Their numbers are low in comparison with the total population of respondents so any difference this will have made is small. If this slight imbalance has had any effect, it may have been to cast a slightly more positive light on the Register and its operation than might otherwise have been the case (since more "satisfied customers" replied). As there was, in fact, no shortage of criticism of any aspect of the Register's functioning, criticisms included here can be read as by no means an overstatement of what the total population of registered relatives is likely to think.

Project Advisory Group

A project advisory group met at Durham University on three occasions during the life of the project. The then OPCS was represented by the Head of the Adoptions Section, and there were representatives, too, of Family Care which runs Birthlink (the Scottish national register) and of the newly established Northern Irish Adoption Contact Register. Several organisations offering post-adoption support provided members: the National Organisation for Counselling Adoptees and their Parents (NORCAP), the West Midlands Post-Adoption Service (WMPAS), Parent-to-Parent Information on Adoption Services (PPIAS) and the Natural Parents' Network (NPN). The social work profession was represented through Durham Diocesan Family Welfare Council and the Northern Region of British Agencies for Adoption and Fostering (BAAF). A number of academics with relevant expertise in research methods and in adoption came from Durham and Newcastle upon Tyne universities. The Department of Health was offered a place and chose to be represented by OPCS, with the exception of the final meeting at which a member of staff from the Department made a presentation concerning the consultation exercise on the draft Adoption Bill. The Grandparents' Federation also had a place on the group, although its representative was unable to attend. This diverse and experienced group included, within the membership listed above, at least three adopted people, at least one adoptive parent, one birth parent and one other birth relative.

This inclusion of direct participants in the adoption "triangle" was considered essential in order to offer a broad perspective on all aspects of adoption. It proved invaluable at certain points in the discussion of how participants should be contacted, how questions should be phrased, and so on. Post-adoption expertise also emerged as an essential element of the advice available to the researchers. Indeed, some regret was felt that the group had not been convened before the research began (it had seemed more sensible to wait until there was something to report) because the letter seeking relatives' agreement to participate in the research went out in a form whereby the envelope was identifiably from OPCS (bearing their frank mark), which may have led some people to think their "link" had occurred, at least until they opened the envelope and saw the University of Durham's headed stationery. One letter of complaint was received to this effect. Any such misunderstanding was profoundly regretted by the research team. The Advisory Group suggested a non-dentifying frank on later correspondence and plain white envelopes. On the positive side, some respondents expressed gratitude at the confirmation that their details were still safely on the Register and were held in correct form.

Additional sources of background information

In order to supplement the information the researchers had gathered by means of the literature review about the context of post-adoption work with birth relatives, it was decided to carry out some telephone interviews with people working in this field. Drawing on issues raised in a recent report (DoH Social Services Inspectorate, 1995), and on a list of key organisations drawn up with the help of Advisory Group members, the following were contacted by telephone: Natural Parents' Network, NORCAP, West Midlands Post Adoption Service, After Adoption – Manchester, After Adoption – Wales, the Post Adoption Centre in London, Barnado's, Hampshire County Council (Adoption Information Exchange), and After Adoption – Yorkshire and Humberside. Questions were asked about matters such as the range of services each organisation provided to birth relatives, the lack of uniformity in post-adoption services nationally, and experience of relatives using the Adoption Contact Register.

In addition, the project research assistant attended a group discussion involving adoption agency representatives and social services adoption staff within BAAF's Northern Region. Similar questions were asked but within a discussion format, allowing certain topics to be expanded upon. Those present included representatives from Newcastle upon Tyne, Middlesbrough, Sunderland, Gateshead, Durham and Cumbria Social Services Departments, the Children's Society, BAAF and Barnardo's.

These contacts also served to triangulate some of the data gathered by means of the questionnaire. For example, agency staff spontaneously mentioned the lack of publicity the Register had received and the fact that most people did not know about it, the level of the fee, and the low number of links achieved. All of these matters also emerged as concerns of Register users.

One further source of background information was ONS itself, both through Adoptions Section staff who supplied information about the number of links achieved over time (see Chapter 6 for commentary on this), and, via them, from ONS statisticians who provided the demographic data on which are based the above comparisons between the Register population and the survey's self-selected sample.

Main method of data collection

The main method adopted for data collection was an anonymous questionnaire (the questions asked are reproduced in Appendix III). In order to preserve confidentiality, all correspondence between the research team and the survey participants was distributed via the office of the Adoptions Section of the then OPCS (now ONS), whose assistance is gratefully acknowledged. Each person on Part II of the Register was given a five-digit numerical identification number by Adoptions Section staff, and it was this number that was subsequently written on the questionnaire (if the person agreed to receive one). Subsequently, it was discovered that six questionnaires had been issued blank, without an identifying number, and these were given numbers in a different series by the researchers. In the event, no stage of the work required Adoptions Section staff to match the numbers back with the names (for example, no reminder letter was sent which would have necessitated identifying who had, and who had not, replied), so the numbers merely facilitated data entry by the researchers and preserved anonymity as far as the research team was concerned.

It was necessary to seek the written consent of relatives on Part II of the Register to take part in the survey, not just as part of good research and data protection practice, but because people would be being contacted for a purpose different from that for which they had entered their details on the Register, as maintained under the terms of the Children Act 1989. A permission letter (stressing confidentiality) with a return slip was drafted jointly by Adoptions Section staff and the researchers, and was sent to all relatives on Part II. Some replies may have been delayed by a localised Scottish postal strike in November 1995 but it is not believed that this prevented anyone from being included who wished to be.

The postal questionnaire

The primary means of data collection was the questionnaire, administered by post to those who had agreed to receive it. This was designed to acquire a mixture of easily codable, quantitative information (including demographic details to ascertain representativeness as against the Register as a whole), and also a considerable amount of qualitative material, obtained in response to open-ended questions. The latter were considered important because the project was concerned with an emotive and sometimes contentious subject, and needed to gather views and opinions in depth. This made the questionnaire rather long. An original idea of replicating earlier work on the impact of relinquishment on mental health was not pursued because the literature review revealed this as one of the better researched areas to date. The aspect of the questionnaire which sought to take the opportunity of gaining a more general picture of birth relatives' experience of adoption and views on increasing openness in adoption practice was kept succinct, following discussion with the Advisory Group, so that the work retained its central focus on the working of the Register itself. Even so, the questionnaire remained rather lengthy, which led to an interesting disagreement between the experienced researchers in the group, who said that no one would complete it, and the post-adoption specialists, who said that a population silenced for so many years would jump at the chance. In the event, the latter were proved right (see comments above on the high return rate), which suggests that birth relatives (and probably some other areas of user feedback) are a "special case" as far as received wisdom on research methods is concerned.

Initially, it was decided to reproduce the questionnaire on one side of A4 sheets only, to allow respondents to give additional information on the back, since it was anticipated that some people would want to write at length. This was later altered in response to postage considerations, which will be discussed later but it did not hinder people from answering fully, enclosing additional letters, and so on.

Pilot stage

The draft questionnaire went through a two-stage piloting process. The members of the Advisory Group were sent an advance copy and prepared comments to be submitted at the first meeting. In addition, those who were based in organisations working with birth relatives also assisted with locating suitable people to pilot the questionnaire. The Advisory Group decided to avoid any loss of people from the main sample by calling only on individuals who were not on the Adoption Contact Register at this stage, even though this would mean that not all questions directly applied to them. It was still considered that they would be able to assist in ensuring that questions were clearly framed and sensitively worded. The representatives from Birthlink, NORCAP and NPN on the Advisory Group each agreed to find ten people who were not on Part II of the Register but who would be willing to complete the questionnaire. The pilot questionnaires were returned by January 1996.

Following each stage of the piloting, changes were made to the questionnaire which, taken together, amounted to reducing its length, clarifying the language used to make it as accessible as possible, and reordering the questions into topic areas with an overall sense of progression. The demographic questions were placed at the end, with a clearer justification for their inclusion, since it was felt that birth relatives (particularly birth mothers) who had felt powerless during the adoption placement experience itself, might once again resent an outside agency (albeit a university-based research team) asking personal questions, some of which might appear to have a judgemental edge or even directly to echo the questions asked when their child was considered for placement. Care was taken to explain in the questionnaire that it was important to be able to check representativeness in order to have the data gathered taken more seriously.

Distribution of questionnaires

It was decided that all questionnaires would go out with return postage pre-paid. As quite a high proportion of them were to be sent overseas, it was intended to apply for an international postal licence to cover the costs of respondents returning completed questionnaires. However, after investigating this option, it was found that the rules on size and weight of enclosure and on envelope size were too restrictive. It took considerable persistence to discover the alternative of International Reply Coupons, which would enable people to avoid return postal charges. This proved to be a very successful and efficient way of overcoming the problem of international postage charges, to the extent that overseas respondents achieved a better rate of return than UK-based participants. (A further factor here was no doubt the higher profile for relatives' rights in certain countries, as mentioned above.) For UK residents, prepaid return labels were supplied under a response service licence with the Royal Mail.

At the first Advisory Group meeting, an ethical question about the return of the questionnaires arose when concern was expressed by some members that, as questionnaires were to have been returned to Southport, Adoptions Section staff would theoretically be in a position to link up people's responses to their actual identities. This could potentially worry respondents and perhaps deter some people from returning the questionnaires, or from being fully open in their replies. It was consequently decided that the reply-paid labels would be addressed to the researchers at the University of Durham, but that respondents should also be offered the option of returning the questionnaire to Southport if they preferred the previously notified arrangement. The return of material direct to Durham meant that the Adoptions Section were not able to check that people had not written identifying details on the questionnaires. This was fully discussed by the Advisory Group, with members of post-adoption organisations feeling strongly that participants should be free to disclose information about themselves if it was their wish to do so, and that this was a wholly different matter from the then OPCS breaching confidentiality about them. This view prevailed, and the covering letter accompanying the questionnaire was adjusted accordingly.

The timescale allowed for replies was made as flexible as possible, with an eventual cut-off date of 15 May 1996 to allow for the analysis of data before the research assistant's contract ended. As mentioned above (in connection with response rates), cost/benefit and ethical considerations meant that no reminder letter was sent. Rather, it was decided to thank all the participants by sending a short summary of the research findings, using that opportunity, also, to remind people of the contact addresses for post-adoption support groups (see Appendix II) in case the research had awoken unhealed memories.

Analysis and presentation of questionnaire responses

Every question asked on the questionnaire, both quantitative and qualitative, has been coded and analysed as a frequency count. This includes those questions which begin with a quantitative element but lead into an open-ended slip question intended to produce qualitative data; each element has been coded separately. All the coded quantitative and qualitative material was keyed into a database. It was then analysed using the Statistical Package for the Social Sciences (SPSS). Frequency counts and percentages were produced, which are reported on below, and some cross-tabulation was carried out, although it did not produce any particularly interesting results and has not been included here. It is possible that secondary analysis of some of the data may be carried out at a later date, for example, in relation to planned further work on the experiences and views of birth siblings.

All frequency counts, when presented as percentages, refer to valid cases, i.e. those who actually answered that question. To make the results easier to read, an indication is always given, too, of the actual number of people who gave that response. (In order to compare differential responses between questions it is necessary to look at the number responding, not the percentage, since the latter relates to the number replying to that question and therefore does not have a constant baseline.) The number responding as a percentage of the whole sample is not shown but can easily be calculated (N = 1,784). All percentages are rounded to one decimal place, and there is a footnote whenever this leads to rounding errors in tables.

Qualitative questions were coded by interpreting the basic component of a comment and categorising it into broad groupings. An example of this is question 42: 'What would you most like to know about the adopted person that you don't know at the moment?'. Comments which indicated a desire to know the sort of people adopted relatives had become – including a wish to make enquiries about their education, employment and marital status – were all grouped into one category under the heading "Personal/current circumstances". Comments where the respondent wanted most to explain how much they cared about the adopted person and/or why the relinquishment took place were grouped into a category as "Love person/explain adoption". As can be seen, sometimes this need to group individual comments into broad and necessarily over-simplified categories meant that subtle nuances were lost. This loss is counteracted, it is hoped, by the inclusion of typical and/or thought-provoking comments as quoted qualitative material throughout this book. Thus the richness of the qualitative data has been preserved but a quantitative measure of the weighting between different types of comment has also been offered. The reader is thus able to see at a glance how typical direct quotes are of responses in general. It was decided, on reflection, not to include numerical identifiers (respondents' code numbers) against the quotes, in case this was seen as a potential source of a breach of confidentiality since the ONS in Southport holds the list matching numbers to names. (Once again, there is absolutely no intention of suggesting that anyone there would wish to work out who said what – it is the principle that it would have been possible which is important.) The disadvantage of omitting the numbers is that the reader is unable to check that the researchers have not repeatedly quoted from the same few people. An assurance is offered that this is not the case and an annotated draft, bearing the numbers, is being held by the Director of the research in case of *bona fide* research enquiries.

Restrictions of timescale

One source of data collection which had to be abandoned when the funded time ran out was the original idea of undertaking a small number of telephone interviews with selected birth relatives, by asking them to call a freephone number in order to preserve anonymity. However, funding has been attracted for a follow-up study which will use this opportunity as its main source of data collection, seeking permission to tape and transcribe the calls in order to subject them to a computerised analysis of discourse. This further study will concentrate on the birth siblings of adopted people who appear, on the basis of impressions gained from the present study, to constitute an interesting and previously unresearched group with particularly strong views (see Chapter 9).

Conclusion

The study consisted of a questionnaire survey of 1,784 relatives on the Adoption Contact Register, representing a 76 per cent return rate and 52 per cent of all those on the Register at the time. The data they supplied were supplemented by contact with specialist organisations operating in the post-adoption field.

With the advice of an immensely knowledgeable advisory group and the skilled administrative assistance of the staff at Southport, the project proceeded remarkably smoothly. All the planned elements were completed, with the exception of a small-scale telephone survey for which additional funding has since been attracted.

As often happens when a wealth of data is generated, its analysis will no doubt give rise to as many questions as it answers and, certainly in the case of this study where the planned year of work was very fully occupied owing to the high response rate, ample scope for further research is revealed in the following account of the major findings. Nevertheless, even as they stand, these findings represent the first ever independently researched data about the workings of Part II of the Adoption Contact Register and they also throw fascinating light on relatives' own views about the wider state of post-adoption provision for birth relatives in England and Wales. It is hoped that they will prove useful in considering how that provision should develop in the future.

4 First impressions of the Adoption Contact Register

Respondents were asked practical questions concerning the channel through which they had heard about the Register, whether they had been affected by the level of fee charged, and whether the application information sent to them had been "user friendly". In addition, they were asked about more personal matters such as their feelings on learning of the Register's existence and their reaction to the style of service offered. All these topics gave rise to thought-provoking responses.

Initial source of knowledge about the Register – the question of publicity

Respondents were asked how they had first found out about the Register (Table 4). It was important to learn how effective both the official and word-of-mouth publicity for the Register had been since this could have implications for reaching future users of the service.

Table 4

Original source of information about the Adoption Contact Register

Source	n	%
Media	533	31.6
Social services/adoption agencies	396	23.5
ONS/Registry offices	72	4.3
Friends/relatives	350	20.8
Post-adoption support	248	14.7
Other public places	81	4.8
Overseas sources	5	0.3
Totals	1,685	100.0
Missing data (non-responses)	99	–

The most common source of information, which had reached almost a third of respondents, had been "the media", a term which here encompasses a wide range of sources, from newspapers and magazines (predominantly those designed for women) to television, radio, and even screen-based information services such as Teletext and Ceefax. Other predominant sources of information had included hearing about the Register from social services or a voluntary sector adoption agency (23.5 per cent), from a post-adoption support group or organisation (14.7 per cent), or from friends or relatives (20.8 per cent). Only 72 people (4.3 per cent), out of the total of 1,784 participants in the study, said they had found out about the service from the providers themselves, the General Register Office or the then OPCS.

This failure of self-promotion by the Register is confirmed by the extremely small number of people in the sample who had seen the poster (Appendix IV) sent out by OPCS in the initial period following the launch of the service. It was distributed to social services departments, voluntary adoption agencies, and other public services such as doctors' surgeries and hospitals. Only 45 respondents (2.6 per cent) remembered having seen it and the vast majority (92.9 per cent, 1,619 people) were sure they had not. (A delegate at the 1996 Post-Adoption Forum conference echoed this with the question: 'Poster? What poster?'). It therefore became meaningless to analyse respondents' views about the design and impact of the poster, although further work, in the form of interviews with key people in post-adoption organisations, brought to light a history of unhappiness with the design chosen by the Department of Health on the grounds that it misleadingly appears to offer "contact" (a theme that will recur below) and that the size of print used gives more visual prominence to adopted people than to birth relatives. Its logo, of two figures with joined hands and outer arms outstretched, also appears to represent unremitting joy rather than a complexity of emotions, and the figures both appear to be male whereas, as could have been predicted, birth mothers are by far the largest group of birth relatives to have registered (2,382 out of 3,404 as at 25 March 1996).

Over three-quarters of respondents (77.1 per cent, 1,355 people) considered that there had been insufficient publicity for the Register. Bearing in mind that the original poster campaign remains the only

Figure 2
Have you seen the OPCS poster publicising the Register?

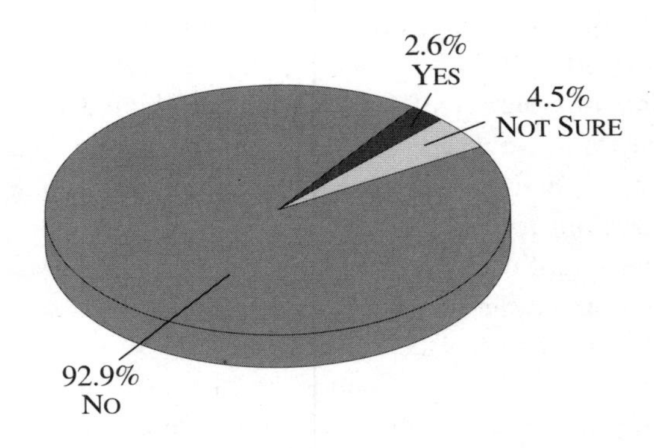

official advertisement the service has received since the Register began, such poor results are worthy of note and mean that any future publicity would need to take a far more proactive approach in order to be effective. Almost all respondents (94.7 per cent, 1,658 people) thought publicity should be repeated periodically. Further comments which people took the opportunity to offer showed an acute awareness of the general lack of promotion and its adverse implications – notably the probable effect on the success rate of links, and the fact that the lack of publicity added to the nervousness some people felt about their details remaining securely registered:

> '*I realised so few people knew about it and even where they did, there was little confidence in its success rate.*' (Birth mother)

> '*I haven't heard a word from them since I registered in 1991. I have seen no advertising for them, in fact. I didn't know if they were still in operation until I telephoned them to see if I was still registered. What does the money go on?*' (Birth mother)

> '*It cannot do what it sets out to achieve if no one is aware of its existence and purpose.*' (Birth mother)

One participant mentioned that, because there was no mass publicity reaching out to all sections of society where birth relatives were likely to be found, the information:

> '*[was available] only to those who make an effort to keep abreast of current events and then only to the literate who look at advertisements, so [it is] somewhat excluding, limiting.*' (Birth mother)

Another summed up what relatives would like to see, and what would be the hallmark of a service confident about itself and what it offers:

> '*Publicise it more! What's wrong with making a TV commercial about it? I think there would be a large increase in the number of people using the Register. Definitely there would be more reunions.*' (Birth mother)

Participants in the study suggested a number of places where publicity could be targeted. Almost half of the thousand or so who responded to this question (46.8 per cent, 469 people) would have liked to see more widespread use of the media. Once again, this covered a broad range – from print to television. (One person attending the Post-Adoption Forum conference in 1996 considered that a storyline in a popular soap opera was the surest way to attract attention to any social issue.) Two-fifths (40.5 per cent, 406 people) felt there should be a publicity campaign in all buildings with public uses such as post offices, hospitals and doctors' surgeries, schools and colleges, and Citizens Advice Bureaux, as well as other heavily frequented locations such as supermarkets and on public transport. A poster or billboard campaign and a mailshot were also suggested. Seventy-nine people (eight per cent) particularly requested publicity overseas – many of the overseas participants had had difficulty finding out about the service – and several people proposed placing information on the World Wide Web. Any publicity efforts would need to be regularly repeated and updated, so that fresh people would see them, not only because there will continue to be, for some time to come, new generations reaching adulthood who could potentially benefit from the service, but also because some people who either did not want to use the Register in the past, or who could not have coped with it at an earlier stage, may now be ready to use it.

However, any renewed publicity drive would need to be preceded by a very careful rethinking of the service provided by the Register since, as the findings reported below will reveal, (i) there has been some misunderstanding of its purpose with even its name being misleading (it does not actually offer a "contact" service) and (ii) it does not currently offer all aspects of the service that people say they want. Clearly, this is not a sound basis for an immediate marketing operation.

ONS staff accept that there is a general lack of awareness of the Register's existence and purpose amongst its potential users and intend, in the financial year 1997/98, to explore any available effective and resource-efficient means of promoting the Register (personal communication with ONS Adoptions Section). The fact that recent media interest in the reunion of the prominent politician, Clare Short, with her adopted son coincided with substantially increased enquiries about, and applications to, the Register would seem to confirm that there is scope for further publicity.

Initial reactions to the Register

Once people had learnt about the existence of the Register, what were their emotional reactions to finding out about the service it offered? Over three-quarters (78.3 per cent, 1,364 people) described a feeling which was predominantly positive or hopeful. A few (6.7 per cent, 117 people) felt largely surprise, while one in ten had mixed feelings. Only 78 people had an initially negative or disappointed reaction.

Of the positive comments, many related to the fact that the birth relative's need to know about the adopted person had finally been acknowledged and legitimised by the setting up of the Register:

> '*To hear a government department has accepted that birth parents and adoptees have understandable needs, that were ignored by a government department in the past, put an official stamp on my feelings being normal. It is proof to society that it has moved on and changed its attitudes. I tell my friends with pride that I am on it; it gives me self-esteem.*' (Birth mother)

> '*A door was open that had been closed by bureaucracy.*' (Birth mother)

> '*It was the first official acknowledgement of being a birth mother.*' (Birth mother)

Some comments, particularly from birth mothers, reflected a sense of relief and peace of mind at being able to take some initiative in improving the chances of contacting a long-lost, adopted relative.

> '*It gave me hope instead of despair and helped in my day-to-day well-being. Otherwise, we just have to sit and wait for the adopted person to fight their way through the red tape for any information.*' (Birth mother)

> '*It allows me to talk and open old wounds and try to get them healed properly. This Register has allowed me to talk to people who know where I am coming from – at last we are coming out of the closet.*' (Birth mother)

> '*I have given myself a little peace of mind that I have at least tried something. Made a little effort. I am not trying to sweep things under the carpet or hide.*' (Birth mother)

> '*His birth certificate, his hospital bracelet, reassured me that he was once there. To be able to register his name, as his birth mother, has made a difference to my feelings of hope, that I have been able to do something positive makes it, again, more real.*' (Birth mother)

> '*One thing I did achieve was to lay a ghost. When my son was adopted, I was made to feel guilty, ashamed, wicked, evil. Registering my details, in a sense, was going public, breaking the silence.*' (Birth mother)

> '*Peace of mind because I have been able to make the statement: "If you want to get in touch, I'm here for you".*' (Birth mother)

Ten per cent of those answering this question (175) described having had mixed feelings about the Register. Many of these were torn between, on the one hand, their relief and excitement at having been given an opportunity to register their willingness to be contacted and, on the other, their fear and uncertainty about the possible implications:

> '*Uncertainty – whether to let sleeping dogs lie – but if my child, now a woman of 29, ever wants to find me, she has that right. Afraid of the reaction if we ever meet.*' (Birth mother)

> '*I was both relieved and afraid: relieved that I now had a choice to contact, and afraid of what I might find.*' (Birth mother)

Some comments were forthcoming from birth mothers who had "made a new life" and who now felt vulnerable, knowing that they were opening up not only themselves (both socially and emotionally) but also their new families to contact and all that it might imply:

> '*Vulnerable because the Register gives the adopted person "instant" access to my address.*' (Birth mother)

> '*Dealing with these kind of things opens up old wounds and so, by just registering, I still wonder if I should rake up the past, or let things rest.*' (Birth mother)

> '*I feel frightened about hearing from the Register about my son and would have to think hard about taking it any further. I would be afraid of it harming my family life.*' (Birth mother)

The question of the assistance that counselling and support services might offer with such fears and mixed feelings, were they to be made more readily available, will be returned to below.

Although only 78 respondents reported an initially negative reaction to finding out about the Register, the number of detailed statements with a negative slant was higher because these blurred into people's overall experience of being on the Register over time (which will be returned to in later sections). Negative comments in this part of the questionnaire chiefly relate to disappointment with the limited nature of the Register. Some people had misunderstood the purpose of the Register, thinking that an "Adoption Contact Register" would actually make contact with the adopted person, either just to notify him or her that the relative had registered or in an intermediary role:

> '*I thought that they (ONS) tried to find adopted children and let them know that birth parents were trying to find them.*' (Birth mother)

> '*I thought the Register would search for and let her know of my wish to make contact with her. I felt that I had been misled.*' (Birth mother)

> '*I thought I would get help to find her, but I have had nothing. This*

> *has hurt me. I feel it is a case of pay your money and take a chance.*' (Birth mother)

Others felt frustrated by the limits of the service as dictated by the current adoption legislation, in that it allows only the placing of a relative's name on the Register, as an indication of willingness to be contacted, and not the disclosure of any information to the relative about the adopted person. It is entirely a one-way communication channel. The relative does not have an equal right to obtain information, as the adopted person can, and this engenders various negative emotions and thoughts:

> '*It's very frustrating that these people [ONS] have all the information at their fingertips and it is not allowed to be disclosed. I feel very upset that everywhere I go I come up against a brick wall.*' (Female sibling)

> '*I feel it is very inadequate and extremely restrictive. As a relative, I have questions too.*' (Female sibling)

> '*I feel frustrated by cost and time and red tape.*' (Female sibling)

> '*[It] appears reactive rather than proactive and basically dormant and passive.*' (Birth mother living overseas)

> '*The system is one way – a too naïve concept – not proactive enough.*' (Birth mother)

Thinking about contact – at the beginning

Two-thirds of the respondents (66.7 per cent, 1,182 people) reported that it was finding out about the service provided by the Register which actually allowed them to think for the first time that the longed-for contact with an adopted relative might be a possibility:

> '*Most surprised at existence of the Register considering 40 years ago, my sibling was threatened with imprisonment if we attempted to find our brothers and sisters.*' (Female sibling)

> '*It appeared to me that perhaps the adoption agencies had finally realised that not only closed adoptions were inhuman, but also that they did not work. The closed adoption process violates civil liberties.*' (Birth mother living overseas)

> '*This Register was my tunnel, perhaps with a light at the end.*' (Birth mother)

However, the realisation of the possibility of contact may bring about some complicated emotional issues which will need resolving. Prior to going on the Register, a birth relative can imagine that they are being sought but have not yet been found. Once details are in place, however, this changes:

> '*Before, you could always hope they are trying to trace you but once on the Register if no contact is made, the hope is lost.*' (Birth mother)

> '*It is easy to rationalise that your child cannot find you but not that they don't want to.*' (Birth mother)

As will be discussed below, such considerations can be seen as a further argument for the need for a counselling-based approach, as this would allow people to talk through all the implications of registration, prior to making a decision whether or not to proceed.

Fees

As was mentioned in Chapter 2, existing adoption law gives the Secretary of State the power to prescribe the level of the fee to be charged to those who make use of the Adoption Contact Register. The current fee remains at the same level at which it was set when first introduced in 1991. The public expenditure ethos underpinning it is that the cost of administering the Register should be recouped from those who avail themselves of it. The fact that it is more expensive to process an application from a relative applying to register on Part II than one from an adopted person placing their name on Part I (because of the additional need to provide evidence of relationship and the complications involved in this) has been reflected in a differential level of fees being set. A relative is charged £27.50 and an adopted person £9.50.

Those who operate the Register are aware that the fees charged are controversial in a number of respects but do not foresee any change in the general approach taken, given the prevailing constraints on public spending (personal communication with Adoptions Section of ONS). Post-adoption groups have commented negatively on the existence of a fee, the level at which the fee has been set, and the fact that relatives are charged a higher fee than adopted people. All of these points were reflected in individual replies to the questionnaire.

Questions about the fee did not fail to evoke the expected strong reactions amongst some of the birth relatives in this study. Numerically, though, more than twice as many people said they thought the fee they had been charged was fair (63.2 per cent, 1,105 people) as said it was unfair (28 per cent, 490 people), with 154 "Don't knows" (8.8 per cent). Here, of course, it is important to remember the statistical bias in the population responding, in that all these people were already on the Register. Anyone who had been deterred by the existence of a fee, or who could not afford it, would, by definition, have fallen outside the scope of this study. When the questionnaire went on to give an open-ended opportunity to make comments on the fairness or otherwise of the fee, some wider factors came into play and this is where the full force of the criticisms, even from this particular population of respondents, began to emerge.

Indeed, only one respondent volunteered an entirely positive comment about the fee level:

> '*I feel this is very reasonable as your name is on the register for life.*' (Birth mother)

In order to give a flavour of the 673 sets of detailed comments, they have been grouped into categories and can consequently be displayed in quantitative form (Table 5) as well as being illustrated with some fairly typical quotes.

The highest proportion (61.4 per cent, 413 people) of the 673 who took this opportunity to make a further response stated that the fee might well pose a difficulty for any relative who was unwaged or on a low income:

> '*There should be reduced fees for the elderly, the unemployed and those on low incomes. People should not be deterred from using the Register through an inability to pay.*' (Birth mother)

> '*Should people be barred from tracing their lost children if they can't afford the fee?*' (Birth mother)

Table 5

Comments on fairness of fee

View taken	n	%
Costly if no result	77	11.4
Costly for low income	413	61.4
Discriminatory to relatives	47	7.0
Worth it for result	105	15.6
Should be free	31	4.6
Totals	673	100.0
Missing data (non-responses)	1,111	–

Another relative highlighted the vulnerable financial position many birth mothers, in particular, might be in:

> '*Single women number among the majority of relatives searching. They represent the poorer end of society, statistically. Financial hardship is the main reason for adoption.*' (Birth mother)

Others indicated that financial factors had certainly made it harder, in their own circumstances, to decide whether or not to register:

> '*[I had to] rationalise the use of hard-to-save money, for what I believe [to be] a very selfish reason.*' (Birth mother)

> '*I am looking for two of my relatives, but could only afford to put one on the Register.*' (Female sibling, meaning that she had put herself on the Register in respect of only one adopted relative rather than both)

There are other circumstances, too, in which people may have to pay more than one fee. For example, a person who was him- or herself adopted may have had one or more brothers or sisters who were adopted into different families and so may need to register on both Part I and Part II of the Register in order to stand the best chance of making contact. In such complex situations, ONS has no discretion to waive any of its charges.

Thirty-one questionnaire respondents volunteered the view that they thought registration should be entirely free. Forty-seven people mentioned their awareness of the difference in fee level between adopted people on Part I of the Register and relatives on Part II, and indicated that they considered the extra cost to the latter to be discriminatory (a point which recurs below). A similar sentiment was voiced by a social worker from a northern adoption agency, at a BAAF discussion session, who also made a link with the socio-historical and social class aspects of adoption:

> 'Adoption is social engineering. Adoptees are far more likely to have money than their birth parents. It is illogical that it is cheaper for adoptees.' (Adoption worker)

More than a quarter of the respondents who volunteered a more detailed response to this question (27 per cent, 182 people) linked the matter of the fee with the result they hoped to achieve – that of contact with the adopted person. Of these, 77 thought the money involved was a lot to pay if there was no result, while 105 said it would be worth paying it if they got the result they desired (but still with some implication that the fee was high).

Whether or not any individual *will* achieve their desired result is, of course, a complete unknown and, in a sense is not the service being paid for. The fee covers the administration involved in checking eligibility and placing a name on the Register, maintaining the Register over time, and contacting anyone who has a link. Whether contact actually occurs is a matter of statistical probability, not of quality of service. Hence there is a fundamental problem in asking people whether, as paying customers, they are obtaining a satisfactory service, and several parts of this book must be read with that consideration in mind. For many, no service will measure up to what they want, unless and until they are given full rights to the information which will lead to the adopted person.

When directly asked, in the next question, whether the fee charged should be equal for birth relatives and adopted people, just over half of those who replied (50.9 per cent, 877 people) said that it should. One in six (16.5 per cent, 284 people) was not sure. Almost a third (32.6 per cent, 562 people) did not consider that the fee needed to be equalised, for various reasons, some of which were elicited by means of another open-ended question. For example, one birth mother made a link with the past and with her present emotional state:

> '*Relatives should pay more – it helps with the guilt.*' (Birth mother)

Of those who volunteered detailed views, 263 people explained why they thought it was correct to charge adopted people less, including for practical reasons – it would bring more adopted people onto the Register, thus making it more successful in effecting links – and for moral reasons:

> '*The fact that no one chooses adoption [i.e. to be adopted in infancy], while the adults concerned had at least some degree of choice, makes the adopted particularly vulnerable and in some cases greatly in need of discovering their origins. It seems fair for the fee to reflect this.*' (Aunt)

> '*No fees for adopted people – they had no choice about being adopted – and now society should put it right.*' (Birth mother)

On the other hand, 179 people made detailed comments about the negative discrimination in the fee levels against birth relatives and a further 128 explained why, in their view, the service should be provided either at no charge or at a reduced charge. Their reasons again included a moral and a socio-political message about the history of closed adoption as social engineering in family life:

> '*[It] should be publicly funded in the interests of promoting the family.*' (Male sibling)

> '*The fee charged should be the same for everyone and I don't really feel we should be charged at all – this is something the state should be making amends for.*' (Birth mother)

> '*Still too high. How can it be justified? The state should subsidise this service since the state imposes the conditions of secrecy in the first place.*' (Male sibling)

The qualitative material shows that there is a greater degree of discontent, and even anger – for some, about fees in general and, for others, about the difference between fees charged to birth relatives and those charged to adopted people – than mere columns of statistics might imply. Those who wrote comments to the effect that the inequality in fees was discriminatory to birth relatives often linked this with the lack of equal rights for birth relatives within the Register system. In effect, relatives are paying more for less because they have no rights themselves to information and, even if there is a "link" between entries on the two parts of the Register, the relative can only wait passively while the adopted person decides whether or not to contact them.

> '*It doesn't seem fair that the relatives pay more when they're the ones expected to sit back and wait for things to happen.*' (Female sibling)

> '*Such inequality discriminates against a group already at a disadvantage regarding rights to information on adopted people.*' (Birth mother)

Others made telling comments about the punitive treatment of birth mothers in the past, together with its continuing emotional cost, and linked the question of the fee with the following:

> '*I felt someone was making a lot of money out of vulnerable, emotional people.*' (Birth mother)

> '*[The difference in cost] really makes me feel that I am being used again by the system.*' (Birth mother)

> '*Criminals are given better priority than people like me who made a mistake and pay for it for the rest of their lives.*' (Birth mother)

Some people felt it was unfair to be charged such a high fee for a service with no guarantee of success. One sibling suggested being charged a nominal fee to register one's details and then:

> '*a further charge if successful.*' (Female sibling)

Another sibling would have liked to have been able to find out prior to paying the registration fee whether his sister had also registered, since:

> '*It would have been helpful if I could have found out if this was the case before I paid my fee for registering. Money was tight at the time.*' (Male sibling)

Despite this negative feedback, over three-quarters of respondents (77.6 per cent, 1,370 people), reported that the level of registration fee had not made them think twice about placing their details on the Register. It must be remembered once again, though, that this is a biased sample: these are the people who *did* go onto the Register. Those who had been deterred by the cost, or by any other aspect of the system in operation, were, by definition, not amongst the respondents so they remain an unknown quantity in every respect. In fact, one in five (20.7 per cent, 366 people) did say that the level of the fee had made them think twice, so it is perhaps likely that substantial numbers of others were deterred completely. (ONS has kept no record of the number of forms sent out but never returned, which would have provided a degree of supporting evidence for or against this hypothesis. Consideration might usefully be given to doing this in future since it would provide interesting data.) Nevertheless, over half the respondents in this study (52.9 per cent, 938 people) placed their details onto the Register immediately they heard about it, rising to seven in every ten respondents (70.3 per cent, 1,247 people) who applied within a month. Responses to this section of the questionnaire, then, may be saying less about money than about the deep need for services for birth relatives who choose to try and make contact with an adopted relative, whatever the difficulties or disincentives involved. A far smaller but interesting group of 158 people (8.9 per cent) took over a year to make the final decision to apply. One could speculate that some of these might be amongst the people who were most ambivalent and who might, therefore, welcome a linked counselling service which could talk them through the pros and cons of registration and potential contact for all parties involved, and/or amongst those who found it difficult to raise the money to pay the fee.

One change which ONS has been able to make to reduce the expenditure involved for relatives in placing their names on the Register is to cease the requirement to furnish copies of birth or marriage certificates as evidence of relationship. It is now treated as sufficient for the particulars of the birth or marriage to be specified in the application (provided it took place in England or Wales). This flexibility in administering the Register is welcomed.

The information booklet

One area of positive feedback was that almost everyone (98.4 per cent of respondents, 1,634 people) felt that the booklet, *Information for Adopted People and their Relatives* (ACR 110), had been either easy or reasonably easy to understand. Only 26 people expressed any difficulty with the booklet for themselves. Improvements are always possible, however, and, in response to a subsequent question, 70 people could see some potential difficulties with the booklet which might affect other people if not themselves. Fifty of these felt the language might be too complicated. One birth mother asked whether the document was available in different languages, while others commented on its style:

> '*Very formal/official style and layout – the print is very small. It's not very user-friendly.*' (Birth mother)

> '*I need a concise detailed explanation of what happens and how it operates. I felt slightly let down.*' (Male sibling)

Other requests for particular information quoted below, together with other sections of these findings, suggest that some relatives continue to believe the Register will take a different role from the one it has in reality, and that it will actively search for an adopted person. One could, of course, argue that they believe this because they want and need to believe it, and not because the booklet is necessarily misleading. In the light of this finding, however, there is reason to propose that a key purpose of the booklet is to convey in the clearest possible terms, using modern design techniques as appropriate, what the Register can and cannot do for relatives, the obvious restrictions in its function, and what other services are available elsewhere. This is especially necessary while the Register retains its misleading name as an adoption "contact" register. Arguably, and ironically, one of the booklet's main aims has to be to explain that the Register does not do what its name appears to suggest:

> '*I think it should be stressed that putting one's name on the Register does not necessarily lead to contact. It should be stressed that both sides must be willing to make contact before it is made.*' (Birth mother)

Although the booklet does already make clear mention of this fact, the explanation constitutes only a small part of a lengthy document, which deals with a number of difficult issues, and it may be overlooked or not absorbed. Over and above this, of course, the key role of the booklet is to explain how the system works so that people can make an informed choice whether or not to register, with a good understanding of what happens to the details they provide:

> '*I don't know how matches are linked – it feels a bit sterile to think that someone in front of a computer matches details of people's lives. Is there more information we could be asked to give to help the process?*' (Birth mother)

Some people also need more complex information, such as what to do in situations where there is more than one adoption involved:

> '*I feel very confused about Part I and II of the Register. If my brother doesn't realise that he needs to be on both, we may never find each other.*' (Female sibling)

This last comment echoes the confusion of some other siblings. The booklet seems to imply that there is a clear cut division between those people who are birth relatives and those who are adopted people, whereas, in fact, it is not uncommon to be in both categories:

> '*It does need to take into account the fact that one can be adopted and a relative.*' (Female sibling)

The result can be that two adopted people who had one or both birth parents in common (or, in fact, any other birth relationship) may both register on Part I, as adopted people seeking links with relatives, but not be put in touch with one another because neither is registered on Part II as a birth relative. (NORCAP had such a case in 1995, for example.) This complication needs careful explanation and is a particular pitfall for those who do not know there is another adopted person in their birth family. Since adopted people may know next to nothing about their birth family – often only the bare facts about their birth mother – they are highly likely to lack this information. Similarly, two people who are related but who do not know one another (say, for example, two siblings of one adopted person, both of whom grew up in care but separately from one another, or children of those siblings) could both be registered on Part II as birth relatives of the adopted person and not be put in touch with one another. As family relationships grow more complicated as a result of unmarried parenthood, high divorce rates and serial relationships, and as taking children into public care continues to break birth family links at the same time as adoption has come to be more commonly used to find families for children in care, these kinds of complications are likely to proliferate. It may be that relatives, on applying to register, should be asked whether they also want to be linked with anyone seeking the same adopted person as them and that all other possible links *across* Part I and *across* Part II should be considered. Those who are seeking a link might be very happy to find a family member, even if it is not the one they first thought of seeking.

The other 20 people who criticised the booklet considered that it was hard to understand – to "take on board" perhaps – because it covers an emotionally difficult subject. Particular clarity is needed because messages which would normally be easily understood may become distorted as, for example, birth mothers struggle to come to terms with long buried, deep-seated emotions in relation to the adoption experience:

> '*Scared that I was opening up a very painful part of my life that I thought was closed to me for ever.*' (Birth mother)

> '*I am of course having to deal with flashbacks and panic attacks as blocked memories make themselves known.*' (Birth mother)

One further concern is that more than half the respondents (51 per cent, 903 people) reported not having been aware of the list of organisations available to provide advice and counselling which is contained in the booklet. Since the Register is not directly connected with any counselling service, and yet is positively promoting contact – which is known to be associated with heightened emotions and unresolved issues from the past – this is rather worrying. It is impossible to know whether readers of the booklet missed the list, deliberately ignored it (because they felt they did not need it), saw but did not absorb it (for example, because of their own emotional state or the amount there was to take in), or did not read right to the end of the booklet. Perhaps the list of external counselling and advice services could be more clearly "flagged up" in an earlier section.

Finally, there are some suggestions which might be more "user-friendly", mainly arising from discussions about the research, for example, following conference presentations. A summary page with the main "bullet" points could perhaps be added to the booklet. This would be particularly helpful to those members of the public who may be unused to reading official material and to those who, judging from the above, are likely to miss key points within a closely printed format. A single sheet explaining the Register in broad terms would be cheaper to produce than the full booklet and could be distributed far more widely. It should have a tear-off slip which could be sent direct to Southport to request fuller documentation. At present, it is necessary to write a letter which, in itself, can be a disincentive.

At the time of writing, ONS staff are in the process of revising the application forms to the Register, with the intention of making them shorter and more user-friendly. They are keeping the design of booklet ACR 110 under review and are open to concrete suggestions for improving it (personal communication with ONS Adoptions Section).

Help with understanding the Adoption Contact Register

Two-thirds of respondents (67.3 per cent, 1,152 people) had had no assistance beyond the information booklet with understanding the operation of the Register. The largest contributors of help were the then OPCS itself (10.5 per cent, 180 people), friends and relatives (11.5 per cent, 197 people), and support groups, post-adoption centres and adoption agencies (7.6 per cent, 131 people). A small number of people specifically mentioned help from other sources such as Citizens Advice Bureaux (14), solicitors (five), therapists (two), St. Catherine's House (two) and the Salvation Army (one). A need may well exist for more help and support.

General service: experience of ONS staff

There was a general impression, gleaned from comments throughout the questionnaire responses, that ONS staff were highly efficient. Where birth relatives' responses divided was between those birth relatives who were comfortable with the rather bureaucratic style with which ONS administered the Register and those who would have preferred a more personalised approach.

On the one hand, a number of birth relatives appreciated the efficiency and competence of the ONS staff:

> '*The Register was extremely thorough in checking certificates, etc., and they were efficient and quick in all correspondence.*' (Birth mother)

> '*I felt relief – that there was somewhere that I could contact and know that my request would be handled in a fair and professional way.*' (Female sibling)

> '*The Register facilitates contact in a confidential, controlled manner.*' (Birth mother)

> '*I think the Register has got it about right. The literature is courteous and businesslike and manages to explain what is potentially a complex matter in simple terms.*' (Birth mother)

Furthermore, some birth relatives liked the anonymity of the service and the way in which it ensures the protection of adopted people's identity until they feel able to facilitate further contact:

> '*The Register provides a discreet but minimal service, which I believe to be entirely appropriate.*' (Uncle)

> '*It gave me the opportunity and chance to make contact with my daughter with the confidence of privacy and consideration for hers and my situation and personal feelings.*' (Birth mother)

On the other hand, some relatives were distressed by the businesslike manner of ONS, in its written communications and on the telephone, feeling that it would be more appropriate for the providers of the service to show a greater awareness of the emotions which may be stirred up by the whole process of registering for possible future contact with an adopted relative. For some birth mothers, for example, contacting an official agency in this connection inevitably brought back memories of the way they felt they were treated by the adoption agency at the time of placement, and they were not the only relatives who would generally have welcomed more emotional support and understanding:

> '*I found the staff rather stand-offish when I made my initial telephone query. The attitude appeared to be one of, you're not entitled or allowed any information, or to ask questions.*' (Female sibling)
>
> '*It is a very officious body and I feel that I am beneath its contempt. It is definitely not friendly in its communication. Its presentation is that of the old adoption agencies, where they hold all the power.*' (Birth mother)
>
> '*I found people involved uncaring and non-committed. Very depressing and very sad.*' (Birth mother)
>
> '*Faceless. Bureaucratic. Not flexible. Unemotional. That is what I think of them.*' (Male sibling)
>
> '*Seems to be a bureaucratic mechanism which doesn't seem well suited to dealing with human relationships.*' (Male cousin)

One overseas user had had a particularly frustrating experience:

> '*I live in Australia and when I first wrote for an application form this was returned to me by surface mail (involving 12 weeks of checking the mail box in anticipation). Maybe this was a clerical oversight, but it certainly indicates that those who operate the service see it mainly as a clerical operation. There is room for improvement in attitude, efficiency and understanding of the importance of its role in the lives of those affected by its operation.*' (Birth mother living overseas)

This woman was not alone in feeling that those employed by the Adoption Contact Register need to be trained to recognise the sensitive nature of the work they are engaged in.

> '*Anyone who works in such a place should be sensitive. Imagine how you'd feel if you'd sent this information and had it sent back with no acknowledgement of the human side.*' (Birth mother)
>
> '*The service could be made to feel more that it's run by people. Now*

> *you get the feeling it is a faceless government department.*' (Birth mother)

> '. . . *to be less functional and to realise people's feelings come into all of this* . . .' (Birth mother)

Some birth relatives had also been in touch with the register run by the post-adoption support group, NORCAP, and volunteered the view that they preferred it. Some even thought NORCAP would be better suited to run the official Register because of the personal engagement aspects of its approach and its belonging to the voluntary sector:

> '*Most government agencies are run on robotic lines and everything has to be black and white. NORCAP is run by people who were themselves adopted as children. They therefore understand the emotions in both the child and birth parents. All the training given to government departments will not instil this experience.*' (Birth father)

> '*Let some organisation such as NORCAP run it. Fund them and give them the resources to do the job. They are not civil servants and know about empathy and caring.*' (Birth father living overseas)

> '*NORCAP has a human face: it's not just a bureaucratic, depersonalised system.*' (Male sibling)

Conclusion

From relatively concrete matters such as publicity, fee levels and the information booklet – all of which raise their own questions for debate – relatives' first engagement with the Register moves quickly on to the issues of organisational style and of the emotional as well as the practical needs of those who are contemplating contact after many years of separation.

In a later chapter (see Chapter 10), a comparison of the different models of register currently operating in Great Britain will be offered which will further explore these issues. There is also additional feedback in the next chapter on comparisons between the Register and other post-adoption services used by relatives seeking to re-establish contact.

5 The decision to register

Respondents were asked a number of questions concerning the process of reaching the decision to register and the impact this had had.

Possible "trigger" factors in the decision to register

Talking to adopted people seeking birth records information (knowledge of their origins) has sometimes revealed "trigger" factors or "catalyst" events which have prompted people to undertake their enquiries at a particular point in their lives. These have included, for example, the birth of a child – because it tends to excite interest in one's own birth, one's genetic heritage and medical history. Haimes and Timms (1985), however, considered from their research that the need to know was so great that it was more a question of what held people back (for example, fear of upsetting adoptive parents) than what spurred them on. It was decided to look, in the present research, at the process operating in birth relatives' decisions to enter their details on the Register.

In the present study, 211 people (12.5 per cent) considered that no particular trigger factor had prompted their decision to place their details on the Adoption Contact Register, perhaps paralleling Haimes and Timms' view that seeking contact is simply a natural desire. The rest all cited one or more reasons (Table 6), though many of these related to a longer-term process than to a one-off event.

Nearly a fifth (19.5 per cent, 330 people) considered that it was simply learning of the existence of the Register from a media source of some kind, rather than any event in their own lives, that acted as a stimulus to register. Slightly fewer (17.6 per cent, 297 people) felt it was something about the adoption experience itself, often the process of coming to terms with losing a son, daughter or other relative through adoption, which had led them to register. Life – or age and stage – factors, more resembling what are typically thought of as triggers or catalysts, included

Table 6
Trigger factors in placing details

Trigger	n	%
Media/knowledge of Register	330	19.5
Adoption experience	297	17.6
Family interest	123	7.3
Finding out about adopted person	97	5.7
Death/age/illness	227	13.4
Life events	272	16.1
Mixture of triggers	134	7.9
No trigger	211	12.5
Totals	1,691	100.0
Missing data (non-responses)	93	–

the illness, increasing age or death of relatives, or the respondent's own illness or ageing (227 overall, 13.4 per cent), as well as life events (16.1 per cent, 272 people) – used here as a blanket term to cover major life changes such as the birth of a subsequent child, moving house, divorce, marriage, other children leaving the family home, retirement, and other milestones which make a considerable impact on people's emotional adjustment. These appear to have included some events which typically bring to the surface memories or thoughts about earlier relationships, and other eventualities which make it "safe" now to search for a lost child (or other relative), for example, when marriage or parenthood responsibilities are over so that there is less risk of disruption should reunion occur, combined with more opportunity for the relative to pursue her or his own needs. In addition to the foregoing, a mixture of triggers was reported by 134 people (7.9 per cent) while 123 (7.3 per cent) were prompted to register by family interest.

An interesting sub-group of 97 people (5.7 per cent) cited finding out about the existence of the adopted person as their reason for registering. These are predominantly siblings, i.e. people who were not party to the original adoption decision and perhaps not even born at the time. They are by no means all young. Some only learned that they had a brother or sister when sorting through family papers following a death. One can only imagine something of the feelings of loss entailed in discovering that a life-long relationship has been missed. Since the Register, even then, offers only a minimal chance of a link, this raises serious questions as to whether legislation should give relatives greater rights to trace and contact adopted people. The needs of siblings in the aftermath of "closed" adoptions have not been the specific focus of any previous research and are only really touched on here, though sufficiently so to argue that they deserve greater attention (see Discussion section, below). Some siblings go to their graves without ever meeting their "lost" brother or sister. By what right, and in whose interests, does their family, and then the state, deny them this opportunity? Are anyone's interests actually served? And is it the denial which whets the interest or is that engendered by psychological or social forces of another kind? This could usefully be the subject of further research, both with siblings and with adopted people themselves.

Some of the qualitative comments respondents made also reveal something about what had prompted them to use the Adoption Contact Register. The following statements originate from people who felt the trigger had been the adoption placement itself and coming to terms with it; these were typically birth mothers who wrote graphically about how they were then and how they are now:

> '*Things were very different in the sixties: when your parents said jump, you said "How high?" I never had any say at all in what happened to my baby. Papers were signed with my name but not by me, and the baby taken out of my arms whilst I was held under restraint. My life has never been whole. The lies I was told, my isolation and inner conflict and pain broke my heart years ago.*' (Birth mother)

> '*Despite knowing at the time of the adoption that she has given up all rights to know anything at all about her child, she can't possibly understand the implications of this decision, made at a time of stress, and although not necessarily regretted, one can't imagine how one will feel about it in ten or twenty years.*' (Birth mother)

> '*It gave me the knowledge that I had made a step towards healing the past, by owning it.*' (Birth mother)

'It helped me to open up even more about my "secret" adopted child – helped me to move on.' (Birth mother)

Reasons for deciding to place details on the Register

Respondents were asked an open-ended question as to why they placed their details on the Register. Almost everyone replied. Responses were grouped into categories and so can be represented in quantitative, tabular form, albeit in broader terms than the original comments (see Table 7).

Table 7

Motive for placing details

Stated motive	n	%
Search for adopted relative	355	20.1
Make details available	655	37.1
Contact with adopted relative	474	26.8
To pass on medical information	15	0.8
Only effective option	185	10.5
Chance to explain adoption	82	4.6
Totals	1,766	99.9*
Missing data (non-responses)	18	–

**rounding error*

It is interesting, and also rather worrying, that one in five people (20.1 per cent, 355) made comments to the effect that their decision to place their details on the Register arose from a wish to be able to obtain an active search for their adopted relatives. As this is not the actual function of the Register, it implies a lack of communication of its aims to a substantial proportion of its users or, perhaps, the triumph of hope over what is stated to be on offer. A further quarter of the respondents (26.8 per cent, 474 people) said their motive for registration was a desire for contact, whilst more than a third (37.1 per cent, 655), and the largest group overall, were perhaps more realistically encouraged by the fact that the Register offered a permanent database within which to place up-to-date details of their whereabouts:

'*I was pleased there was a confidential, central place to register my details should my son wish to find out about me.*' (Birth mother)

'*It offered something permanent. Once I placed my details on the Register, I could rest assured that they would remain there.*' (Birth mother)

One in ten rather resignedly said that the Register was the only option open to them, while two smaller groups had particular messages they wanted to convey to the adopted person: 82 wanted to explain why the adoption had occurred, and 15 had specific medical information that they wanted to pass on. It is sad to reflect that these last two sub-groups were more likely than not to be disappointed in their wish, not least because they might have been able to bring help in the sphere of emotional or physical health to the adopted people they were seeking to contact.

Looking at these stated motives for registration raises the possibility of attempting to divide them into those which were most focused on the relative's own needs and those which were "other-centred" or focused on the adopted person. Of course, this is a crude division since motives are often mixed and the same motive may also serve the interests of more than one person. Nevertheless, given that there is an appreciable difference between someone stating that they want to search for their relative and someone else saying they want to make their details available in case the other person wants to contact them, a division can be suggested between 1,014 relatives who gave an apparently "self-focused" reason and 670 who gave an "other-centred" reason. The 82 who wanted to explain the adoption might have wanted to do so for their own or the adopted person's sake and so have not been classified. This means that at least 670 people were putting the adopted person's interests first in making their decision to register and a further unknown number may have considered that the desired contact would be of mutual benefit. This is a long way from the popular image of birth mothers, in particular, as people who selfishly want to burst back into their adopted offspring's lives, at whatever cost. The next section throws further light on this.

Desired outcome of placing details on the Register

As would be expected, the largest group (42.1 per cent, 739 people) wanted to achieve contact with their adopted relative. (Here again, this is a quantitative representation of broad categories of qualitative comments.) Approaching a quarter of the sample (24.2 per cent, 425 people) wished actively to find their relative and roughly one in 16 (6.3 per cent) wanted information, whilst 21.2 per cent (373 people) just hoped to make it easier for their adopted relative to find them if they wished. The low number of links actually achieved to date by the Register means that, for many, these hopes and desires will unfortunately not be realised.

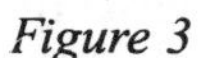

Figure 3

Outcomes desired

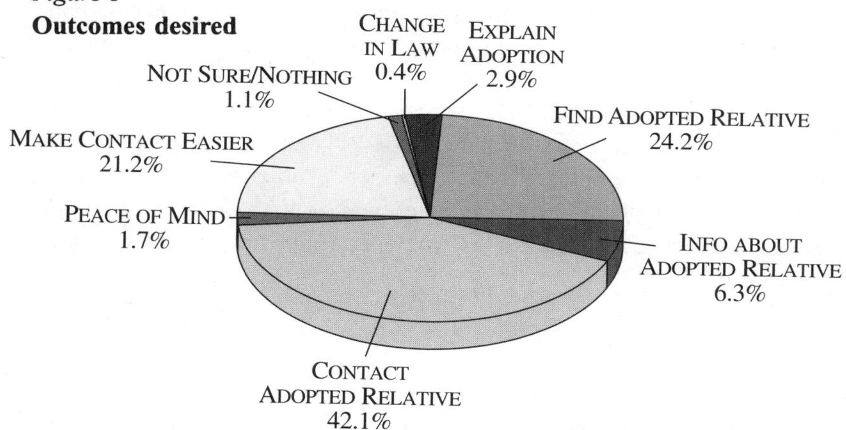

Once again, the selflessness of many birth mothers was evident in some of the comments they wrote, revealing their concern to think of the adopted person's needs (as had been so heavily emphasised in the original placement decision), even whilst admitting their own:

> '*[I have no wish] to try and "power share" with his adoptive parents or have any parenting role or influence at all. I see myself more as a relative who can fill in the gaps for him, answer questions he may have, at the same time learning for myself what sort of person he has become.*' (Birth mother)
>
> '*I understand that I haven't the right to enter his life to cause any upset, but just to know he is safe and well would be wonderful.*' (Birth mother)

For whose benefit details were placed

When asked directly for whose benefit they had placed their details on the Register (Table 8), only one in five reported acting solely in their own interests (21.5 per cent, 382). More than three times as many – seven out of ten of the respondents – were thinking of the adopted person; often jointly with themselves, but sometimes solely or in combination with another relative, or because they believed that everyone involved would benefit from re-establishing contact (totalling 71.2 per cent, 1,262). A further 5.9 per cent were thinking of themselves and at least one relative other than the adopted person. An interesting group of 25 people (1.4 per cent) had in mind the benefit, chiefly, to another relative other than the adopted person, for example, perhaps the birth mother where she herself had not registered. Once again, the "other-centredness" of these replies is striking. This was a "tick-box" question and as many as 145 respondents (8.1 per cent or almost 1 in 12) did not even tick their own box ("yourself"), but one or a combination of the others ("adopted person", "other relative", "other"). This is heavily at odds with the stereotype of birth families as people pursuing their own interests at whatever supposed cost to adoptive families.

Table 8
For whose benefit details were placed

For whose benefit	n	%
Self	382	21.5
Adopted person	111	6.3
Self/adopted person	814	45.9
Adopted person/other relative	9	0.5
Self/other relative	104	5.9
Other relative	25	1.4
Everybody	328	18.5
Totals	1,773	100.0
Missing data (non-responses)	11	–

Availability of counselling and support

In terms of the availability of counselling and support during the period of deciding whether to register, a majority (62.2 per cent, 1,055 people) had lacked anyone to provide this. The largest contributors of support were friends and relatives (24.5 per cent, help provided to 415 people), social services staff (5.2 per cent, 88 people) and support groups, post-adoption centres and adoption agencies (8.4 per cent, 143 people). Only 23 people (1.4 per cent) said they went to a counselling service and, of course, these services are not comprehensively available or known about. As will be seen in a later section, there is a great need for personal support, but it is not currently part of the official system. Even so, 26 people (1.5 per cent) said they had had support from the Adoptions Section of the then OPCS at this stage in the process.

ONS staff kindly monitored the nature of the 90 telephone calls received from relatives during one fortnight in January and another in May 1996. (The telephone monitoring questions are reproduced at Appendix V.) This exercise revealed that despite being untrained in this regard, they are already called upon to go beyond giving out purely factual information over the telephone, for example, when callers are in distress or need to discuss the procedure – as it affects them – in considerable detail. Four calls lasted for more than a quarter of an hour, three callers were in a particularly heightened emotional state, and four were left dissatisfied because ONS could not divulge information about the adopted people they were seeking. Thirty callers were advised to ring NORCAP, while a handful needed to contact adoption agencies or the locations of official records. There is evidence, then, that some people are trying to use ONS to discuss matters concerning the tracing of adopted relatives – up to a third of callers had to be referred elsewhere to discuss this – and that registering can be a highly emotional matter.

Services of a third party

Only 13.7 per cent (240 people) had recorded on the Register the name of a third party who would be contacted first in the event of a "link" between the relative and an adopted person on Part I of the Register, despite the use of a third party being offered as an option. NORCAP had the lion's share of such nominations, with 102. This is an interesting overlap in the work of the "official" Register and that of another, voluntary organisation which also runs what is sometimes seen as a rival register, as is the fact that the two organisations publicise each other's services. Other major sources of third parties include friends and relatives (64 people), social services departments and voluntary adoption agencies (40 people), and other support groups (23 people), including the Natural Parents' Network with eight of the questionnaire respondents.

This low take-up rate of the third party option may reflect the fact that, if a birth relative has decided to make themselves available for contact by an adopted relative, they probably consider that they have come to terms with the adoption experience and wish to be as open as possible. Certainly, many of the study participants were keen to reveal their identities to the researchers (as was their right, provided they initiated it), despite their anonymity having been carefully assured, because it was symbolic of reclaiming part of the past which had been hidden away as a result of the secrecy surrounding adoptions. The following comment sums up the shift in attitudes:

> '*The era of stigma and secrecy should be finally abolished, once and for all. Times have changed.*' (Female sibling)

Nevertheless, there is also the possibility that, since the option of nominating a third party is necessarily only briefly referred to in the ONS information booklet, and since the opportunity to talk through the implications is not routinely supplied, some people may have missed or misunderstood it, or not thought it through in relation to their own circumstances. As will be seen in a later chapter, there may be a tendency for relatives to under-estimate what is involved if a "link" does occur, which implies that more people might benefit from third parties than currently use them.

The emotional impact of registering

Over two-fifths (41.5 per cent, 696 people) described the emotional impact of registering as positive. However, a quarter of the respondents (25.4 per cent, 427 people) felt it had been a negative experience and/or quite frustrating. A further 13 per cent (218 people) had mixed feelings.

Certainly, the process of a relative placing their name on the Register and, particularly, of achieving a link, can give rise to very strong emotions.

> '*The whole thing is a psychological minefield of guilt, secrecy, guilt.*' (Birth mother)
>
> '*I thought I was prepared for how emotional it was – my friend warned me – but it was much, much harder than I realised. It stirred up those very unhappy memories, forgotten, buried guilt, shame, everything. And mine [link] was a success. I wonder how I would have coped if it had failed.*' (Birth mother)

At the risk of repetition, this once again leads into the argument for providing a counselling facility:

> '*It is an emotional roller-coaster and even if the relative feels elated, the initial contact can be an anticlimax or bring new surprises. A support network is really vital, to help smooth the ride through a sea of emotions.*' (Female sibling)
>
> '*Talking really does help – every situation is different but the fears and anxieties seem to be the same.*' (Birth mother)
>
> '*Once contact is made, it brings out feelings that may have been suppressed for 30 years or more and everyone needs some help to come to terms with the lost years.*' (Birth mother)

Conclusion

Questions asked in this section of the survey revealed a natural desire for information and contact, much as has emerged from earlier studies. A high proportion of relatives registering had in mind the adopted person's needs as well as their own, considering that the right to information flowed both ways. Very few relatives acted solely in their own interests. This belies the stereotype of birth relatives as people who are likely to disrupt the stability of adopted people and of their adoptive families for selfish motives.

Even the decision by a relative to place his or her name on the Register can start up "an emotional roller-coaster" and yet few had exercised the option of recording the name of a third party to be contacted first in the event of a "link". A majority lacked counselling and support through this stressful process.

6 Outcomes of involvement with the Register

The most concrete outcome of registration was, of course, whether or not relatives on Part II of the Register had achieved a link with an adopted person on Part I. Those who had had a link were asked about this experience, and all respondents were invited to comment on their level of satisfaction with the Register, what else it might have offered them, and what they most hoped for in the future.

Length of time on the Register

Many of the respondents had been on the Register for rather long periods, given that it was only established in 1991. Over a third (37 per cent of respondents, 653 people) had had their personal details on the Register for between two and four years, and a further 28.7 per cent (508) had been registered for over four years. Despite this, the actual number who had been contacted to inform them that they had had a link (i.e. that their details had been passed on to an adopted relative) was minimal.

Numbers having achieved a link with an adopted relative

Only 72 people, or roughly one in 25 of those in the sample (4.1 per cent), had actually had a link through the Register. (This is a little higher than the roughly three per cent rate of links on the Register as a whole. See Figures 4 and 5.) Since achieving a link is the sole purpose of registration and since the research reported here was, at one level, an independent evaluation of a service for which people had paid, this fact is worth dwelling on. It represents, at least to date, a very low chance of any particular individual obtaining a link. This fact should arguably be reflected in any further advertising of the Register (should such be planned), and in any consideration of whether the fee level is fair, although it would be ironic if advertising the low number of links to date prevented the one thing which could raise it in the future, i.e. more registrations of new people. On the other hand, the odds are better than playing the lottery and better than random, which would be around one chance in a hundred given the estimated number of adopted people in the population and the numbers on both parts of the Register. Factors influencing the better than random chance of a link may include the omission from the equation of those step-parent and other in-family adoptions where there has been no secrecy, and the fact that birth mothers and their adopted offspring from the peak years of adoption are tending to look for one another in greater numbers than other groupings. The rate of links has been fairly constant throughout the life of the Register (Figures 4 and 5) and will only rise significantly if considerably more people join both Part I and Part II.

The irony of the low success rate is further compounded by the fact that post-adoption organisations report some adoption agencies as arguing, in seeking to justify their own lack of post-adoption provision, that relatives now have the Register to call on and should be content

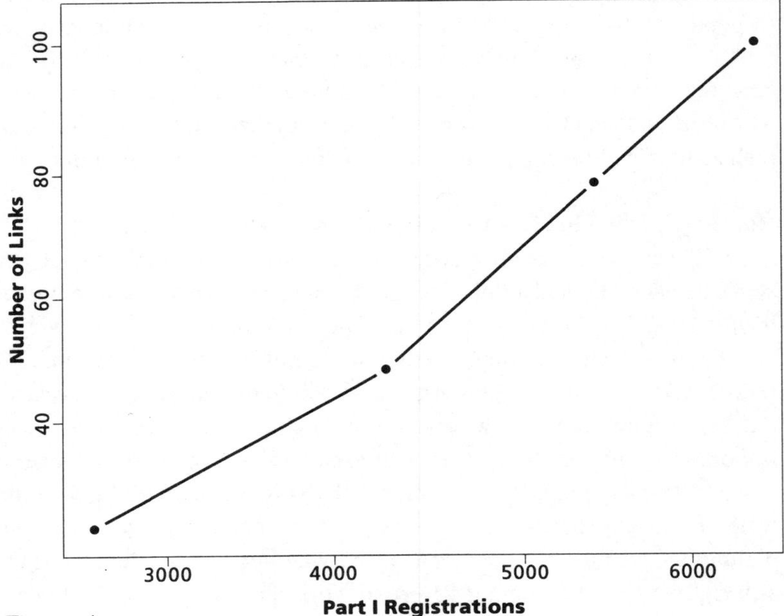

Figure 4

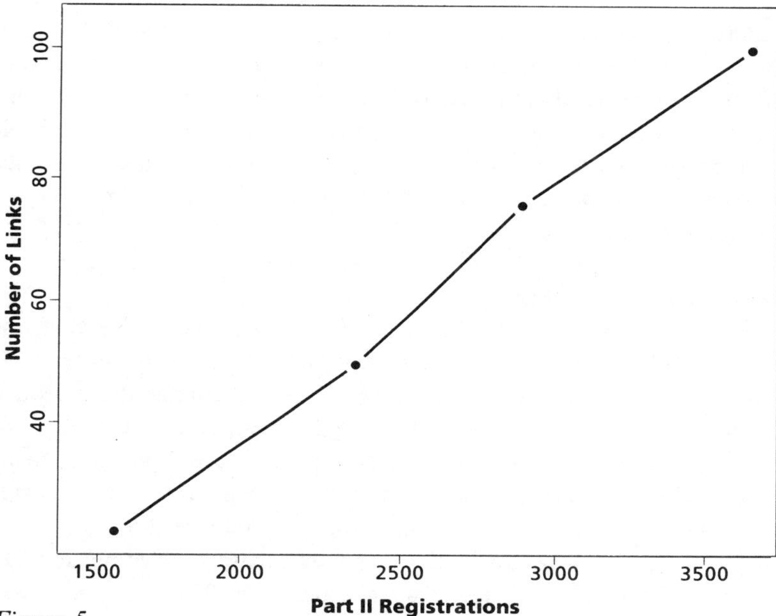

Figure 5

with that. As a result, some post-adoption workers who initially campaigned for the Register reported to the researchers moments of self-doubt in which they wondered whether it has actually been an impediment to relatives' desire for contact, rather than a help. On the other hand, the Register is now in existence and this research will show that it is valued by the majority of respondents as at least offering them something (see below). Activists therefore generally adopt the positive stance of seeking ways to make the Register work more effectively whilst also ensuring that adopted people and their relatives know about other channels for trying to make contact.

One small point to note about the operation of the Register is that a name is not removed following a link unless this is formally requested. The reason for this is that, in the case of the adopted person, there could be a further link with another relative at a later date. For a birth relative it would seem to serve less purpose, since each registration is for one named person (any relative seeking two or more people must pay additional fees accordingly). However, the Register does work to a user-initiated model and it would perhaps be odd for ONS staff to start removing one set of registrations from it (those of birth relatives with a link) without specific instruction to that effect. There are also people still on the Register (one of whom wrote and declined to take part in the research) who have achieved a link through other means but have not removed their names.

Experience of the link

Of the 72 respondents to the questionnaire who had had a link, the majority (42 people, 58.3 per cent) reported it as a positive experience. (In this sub-section, the analysis of results is in the unfamiliar territory, as far as this study is concerned, of dealing with quite small numbers. Throughout this sub-section, results are, therefore, less likely to be applicable to the total population of relatives on the Register or outside it, and percentages are a less helpful representation of the figures than in the rest of the book. Qualitative comments, however, continue to carry their full force of feeling and personal experience.) This sub-group of 72 constitutes an over-representation of people with links as against the Register as a whole, but we do not know whether it also over-represents those who had had a good experience of the link. The finding that most links were positive is supported by the limited amount of other available literature (see Chapter 2).

Just over a third of respondents with links (26 people) had had a mixed reaction, largely to situations where the initial contact was satisfactory but where, as time went on, it became less frequent or did not proceed according to their expectations. Four people felt there was too much pressure to meet before they felt totally prepared for the contact. Many of these less than completely positive responses would appear to indicate that reunion is a process, not an event, and that, as the literature review revealed, it requires careful handling. These might have been situations in which the provision of some form of personal support or counselling – in the period leading up to and following the link, and throughout the process of contact – might have helped relatives to be better prepared for pacing their involvement, modifying their expectations, and anticipating the stages that were likely to be involved, for example, the end of the "honeymoon" period which practitioners say can occur early in contact.

Detailed comments offered by respondents on the linking process highlight how birth relatives had tended to under-estimate the emotional impact of hearing that they were actually going to be closer to linking or reuniting with an adopted relative:

> '*I didn't anticipate the trauma involved. I thought because I've wanted this for so long it would be easy. It's not.*' (Birth mother)

A number of relatives gave feedback indicating that they did not feel adequately prepared for the experience of a link and backing the hypothesis that support would have helped. They would have preferred to have been informed personally about the imminent issuing of their details to the adopted person before this was done, and to have had the chance of some support and advice during the waiting period. Being sent a letter felt inadequate:

> '*Sending the name and address off without any previous consultation, seems irresponsible.*' (Birth mother)

> '*I am not sure I had enough support in place. Contact by letter can be difficult. Personal contact would be much easier to handle.*' (Birth mother)

> '*I would hope that at least a phone call could be made as a letter is such an impersonal way to be told.*' (Birth mother)

> '*I didn't like the form on which you were advised your name and address has been sent to the adopted person. Very cold! It would have been nicer in a letter; it would of course be a very short one but 100 per cent better.*' (Birth mother)

> '*I would have liked personal contact on what might happen next, with some personal support available throughout the process, i.e. telephone contact with a sympathetic and sensitive person dealing with both parties. It is one thing filling up the form; it is quite another dealing with the emotional shock of a real person out there with your name and address, who could arrive or phone anytime.*' (Birth mother)

Help desired with the contact process

Returning to the full sample of respondents, most people, of course, could only speculate what a link would be like but their views are still valuable and, in fact, accord with those expressed above. When asked whether it would be a good idea to have help available in the event of the adopted person making contact, over three-quarters (76.1 per cent; 1,344 people) thought that it would. Fewer than one in ten (9.5 per cent, 168 people) felt they could cope alone. A quantitative categorisation of the further comments respondents made, as to their reasons for feeling the way they did, indicates that seven out of ten (71.8 per cent, 1,003 people) thought support would be required because it would be a very emotional time. Most of the remainder (18.1 per cent, 253 people) considered that whether or not to have help should be a personal decision, depending on the needs of the individual. Just 53 birth relatives (3.8 per cent) implied that it would be a private matter in which they would not want others involved, which presumably need not rule out help being available to other people who might want it or to this group, should they change their minds.

Trying other methods of contact

Given that most people had not achieved a link through the Register, it is to be expected that they would have pursued other possible avenues to find the adopted person. Almost half the respondents (48 per cent, 844 people) had tried to make contact by one or more other methods, before or alongside the Adoption Contact Register. The most popular alternative methods were: making their own enquiries (29.4 per cent, 517 people); entering details on another contact register such as NORCAP's (18.2 per cent, 319 people); the use of a post-adoption service (9.5 per cent, 166 people), other support group (12.1 per cent, 212 people) or adoption agency (11.3 per cent, 202 people); employing a private investigator (4.9 per cent, 86 people); and even approaching media sources, such as television programmes like Cilla Black's *Surprise, Surprise,* or newspaper contact pages (1.7 per cent, 31 people).

Respondents were asked whether any of these alternatives had provided a service closer to what they required than that offered by the Adoption Contact Register, and, if so, in what way. Over 300 people

Table 9
Advantages of other services

Advantage	n	%
Tracing/access to information	112	34.1
Advice/counselling	86	26.2
Feedback/presonal service	72	22.0
Letterbox service	21	6.4
Intermediary	20	6.1
Contact with adopted relative	16	4.8
Cheaper	1	0.3
Totals	328	99.9*
Missing data (non-responses)	1,456	–

* *rounding error*

(18.39 per cent of all respondents, 328 people) gave reasons for preferring another service (see Table 9). The rest did not reply. This was an open-ended question (there were no boxes to tick), so these are respondents' own suggestions, grouped here into categories.

Factors mentioned included: the availability of tracing, letterbox and intermediary services, and/or disclosing or non-disclosing information; the opportunity to obtain counselling and advice; a more personal service, with regular feedback informing people of where they were in the process and of any progress; and, for a few, greater success in actually contacting the adopted person. These points will be returned to in more detail below, in the context of recommendations for change. One person said the preferred service was cheaper.

Desirability of a counselling service

When asked whether counselling or support services should be made available as part of the service offered to relatives by the ONS in operating the Adoption Contact Register, the response was overwhelmingly positive. A very clear majority (82.5 per cent, 1,451 people) said they would like to see in-built counselling. Only six per cent (105 people) gave a negative response and 11.5 per cent (203 people) were not certain.

Some of the latter would perhaps be wary of an inclusive service which was not optional or which they thought might become too intrusive in their personal or family life.

A number of profound comments described the intensity of what was involved in recontacting an adopted person after a number of years, or in thinking about doing so, and, together, they constitute a strong case for counselling to be available to assist people with the whole experience. Comments came both from those who had achieved a link and from those who had not:

'*I lost two babies and found two adults.*' (Birth mother)

'*We would be strangers even though blood relatives.*' (Birth mother)

ONS staff acknowledge that the study reported on here has demonstrated a demand for advice and guidance prior to registration and also following a link (personal communication with Adoptions Section). However, they remain of the view that this kind of help is best provided by an experienced adoption worker or other counsellor and not by legislating for a change in the service provided by the Registrar General. Furthermore, any addition to that service would inevitably re-open the question of the fee charged, which is already controversial even at current levels (see above).

Desired outcomes from the Register

Firstly, people were asked what information they most wanted to receive from, and to send to, their adopted relative. Poignantly, three out of ten of all respondents (30.9 per cent, 532 people) said they would simply like to know anything and everything about the adopted person because no information was available to them at present. Almost half (46.5 per cent, 801 people) wanted most to find out very basic details, such as whether an adopted relative was alive and well and something about the sort of person they had become – what they were like, what they looked like. One in eight (12.5 per cent, 215 people) would have liked to know how the adopted person felt about the adoption.

What virtually half the respondents (48.9 per cent, 836 people) most wanted to be able to tell the adopted person was that they loved them, together with being able to explain all the circumstances surrounding the adoption. Verging on a quarter (23.6 per cent, 403 people) cited, as their main wish, wanting to tell the relation about themselves – what they were like, how they were – and sometimes about any inherited health problems. One in ten (9.9 per cent, 169 people) wanted to convey anything and everything. For some (7.1 per cent, 122 people), the most important message to send was simply that they would welcome contact, should the adopted person ever choose to seek them out. This is, of course, a fundamental purpose of the Register and the very act of registration is a way of sending the message, assuming that the adopted person knows where to look for it (and wants to do so).

Secondly, respondents were also asked what they hoped would be the eventual result of placing their details on the Register. They could tick as many boxes as they liked. There were overwhelming responses in almost all categories: 88.5 per cent (1,574) wanted information about the adopted person; 85.6 per cent (1,522) wanted an exchange of letters and photographs; 74.8 per cent (1,330) wanted to talk on the telephone; 87.3 per cent (1,553) wanted a meeting; 76.8 per cent (1,366) hoped to achieve an ongoing relationship including meetings, and 77.7 per cent (1,381) wished to be informed in the event of the death of their adopted relative. A smaller group (46.2 per cent, 822) wanted an exchange of medical information, perhaps a lower figure because health was not everyone's priority issue at the time or because this option fell so far short of what many were ideally hoping for from the Register. Only 2.8 per cent (50 people) ticked the box to say they were not certain what they hoped would result and 0.9 per cent (16) made no reply about their hopes at this time because they were amongst those who had already had contact.

In one respect, these responses reflect a success of the Register – in that the users of Part II are quite clear why they are using it – but it also shows high hopes (though not necessarily high expectations) which place into stark contrast the low link rates achieved.

Respondents were also free to make their own suggestions of desired results and these included 45 people (2.5 per cent) who wanted to explain the adoption decision to the adopted person; 57 (3.2 per cent) who wanted to achieve a reunion betwen the adopted person and other members of their own family; and 63 (3.5 per cent) who were unwilling to specify the type of contact desired without a process of negotiation with the adopted person. A touching group of 21 people (1.2 per cent) wanted the opportunity to talk to and thank the adoptive parents, giving the lie to perceptions of birth relatives who are bent on disrupting adoptive families.

Expectation of ever seeing the adopted person again

Only one in five (22.2 per cent, 370 people) felt sure that they would see their adopted relative again. Twice as many (46.4 per cent, 774 people) felt certain they would never see the person again and 442, or 26.5 per cent, were not sure. This paints a depressing picture and highlights the importance of what the Register could offer if it were more successful in achieving links. It is worth noting that five per cent (83 people) said they were too young at the time of the initial adoption experience to offer any comment. Most of these people were siblings and some were not even alive or aware of the existence of the other person at the time of the adoption, whilst others had no memory of the circumstances involved. This somehow leaves them in a particular state of uncertainty.

Overall satisfaction rates

Respondents were asked to write about the extent to which the Register fulfilled their needs and why. The quantitative "scoring" of their responses has been achieved by grouping their comments into broad categories. This was not a tick box or a five-point scale question since the researchers did not want to guide people's thinking into over-rigid categories. This means, for example, that respondents were potentially able to express shades of viewpoint.

More than three-fifths of comments (62.6 per cent, 990 people) expressed positives about the Register as a place to leave up-to-date details of birth relatives' whereabouts, so that they could make themselves open to contact whilst also allowing scope for the adopted person to have choices. In this respect, the Register did fulfil a need within the limits of the current law and, for some, it offered all that they wanted:

> '*[I was] pleased there was a confidential, central place to register my details should my son wish to find out about me.*' (Birth mother)

> '*I am glad that any contact would be at his instigation – this seems the right way round to me.*' (Birth mother)
>
> '*Going on the Register created a window for contact which would in no way harm her if she did not also seek contact. There didn't seem to be a safer way of reaching out.*' (Birth mother)
>
> '*I am not actively searching for my son, but I feel secure in knowing that if he is searching for me then I have made it easier for him.*' (Birth mother)

Others felt they had no right to more, but sounded as if they were battling with competing feelings. For this birth mother, for example, it was morally important to stick to her original "bargain":

> '*It would be very easy for me to hire a private detective to make a search, but this would be against the agreement I made when I put him up for adoption.*' (Birth mother)

Of course, it could be argued that the other side of this particular bargain has not been kept since adopted people now have rights to birth records information which birth mothers placing children prior to 1975 were told would be permanently confidential. Social conditions and attitudes have moved on considerably in the interim and, even were more rights to be accorded to birth relatives, those holding strong views against initiating contact would be under no pressure to do so. Furthermore, it cannot be assumed that all those who are cited above as being satisfied with the Register as it stands would necessarily be dissatisfied with the Register were it to change, as is indicated by the majorities who agreed with questions elsewhere in this study proposing increased rights. All that can be read into the above finding is that certain features of the existing system are appreciated, notably the efficient maintenance of a centrally held, confidential register and the element of control over contact which is currently given to adopted people. Other systems which retained those features might be equally appreciated.

Nearly a quarter of the respondents (24.4 per cent, 385 people) were deeply dissatisfied with the service and considered it had been of little help. At one in four, this must be taken as a high level of discontent.

People were frustrated by the lack of results, the poor publicity which compounded the low success rate, and the dearth of communication from the ONS once the registration fee had been paid.

> '*I feel a measure of disappointment at the continuing silence . . . imagining something might have prevented her from using the Register. . . fixating on postal deliveries, anticipating the long awaited letter or phone call . . . willing something to happen.*' (Birth mother)

> '*. . . the paying of the fee to put one's name on a register and then total silence, suggests that anything would be an improvement.*' (Female sibling)

> '*. . . it would be good for the OPCS [now ONS] to regularly report that they have received no details – obviously you hear nothing because there is nothing to report, but the waiting and not knowing is very hard.*' (Birth mother)

> '*I felt let down and dismayed by the lack of response. Later, I accepted that the office was only doing its job and was bound by law not to give me the information I so desperately require.*' (Female sibling)

> '*The Register just maintains a barren silence.*' (Birth father)

Just over eight per cent (8.1 per cent, 128 people) went further in their replies to this question and expressed annoyance that there was no provision for the Register to be more proactive on behalf of relatives, either by giving disclosing details during the link process, as are given to adopted people, or by helping to trace the adopted person:

> '*It could become a more active part of the search for relatives.*' (Female sibling)

> '*The service should be proactive not reactive. [There needs to be the] development of an active role in bringing people together.*' (Male sibling)

> '*I wanted to be able to actually do something constructive. I think it is hard for a relative, especially when it is up to the person adopted to make contact first. It makes you feel helpless and frustrated.*' (Female sibling)

The energetic stance of siblings, reflected above, will be further commented on in Chapter 9. Once again, dissatisfaction was connected for many relatives, whatever their degree of relationship, with a call for increased rights and a change in the law:

> '*The lack of freedom of information is based on out-of-date laws. Information should now be freely available.*' (Birth mother)

> '*The records should be open. There is too much secrecy; these are our blood relatives and we should have the right to know them.*' (Male sibling)

> '*The register is the only link that I have. In reality, it is a toothless tiger because of the government restrictions imposed on it.*' (Birth mother)

Conclusion

Only one in 25 of the sample, or 72 people in total, had had a link with the adopted person with whom they desired contact. This means that many others continued to wait in vain or utilised other methods of seeking contact. Only increased numbers of registrations will improve the statistics significantly.

The majority of links were reported as positive. Once again, support through the process would have helped some people, for example, in pacing events according to their own emotional capacity or in setting their expectations at a more realistic level. The desire for other services, such as information exchange, also began to emerge at this point in the survey. An overwhelming majority of respondents hoped registration would result in a meeting but only one in five had any firm expectation that this would be the case. Nearly a quarter of respondents were deeply dissatisfied with the service provided by the Register and annoyance was expressed that it could not be more proactive. A majority did feel, however, that at least it provided a concrete means of expressing their willingness to be contacted and, for some birth mothers in particular, this encompassed all they felt they had a right to.

7 Potential changes in the operation of the Register

A range of questions was posed about possible changes to the functioning of the Register. These stemmed from three sources: the draft Adoption Bill, respondents' own ideas, and some specific suggestions which had arisen from discussions with agencies active in the post-adoption field. Each of these will be considered in turn below.

1. Changes proposed by government – The right not to be contacted
The questionnaire was designed prior to the issuing of the draft Bill and consultative document, *Adoption – A service for children* (Department of Health and Welsh Office, 1996) which includes a proposal to introduce a measure whereby both adopted people and birth relatives could express the preference *not* to be contacted by all or specified relatives. In designing the questionnaire, the researchers anticipated that the Government might be considering such a measure. A number of relevant questions were therefore posed to survey respondents.

"Non-contact" mechanism for adopted people
Half of the respondents (51.2 per cent of those who answered this question, 49.7 per cent overall, 887 people) agreed that such a measure should be available to adopted people, mainly because they are seen as having a right to privacy, while two-fifths (20.1 per cent) – a sizeable minorty of 349 people – considered that such a measure definitely should not be introduced. It is important to note that three out of every ten respondents (28.7 per cent, 497 people) were uncertain, and that the detailed comments which followed implied some confusion over the meaning of such a measure, despite the care taken to explain it carefully in the questionnaire. For example, as many as 130 people (11.2 per cent) went on to write about adopted people's right to information, which was

virtually the opposite of what was being asked about. A further 201 (17.3 per cent) felt that the contact register was for initiating contact and that, therefore, a "non-contact" measure was a contradiction of its objectives. Some appeared utterly bemused as to why the question was being asked in a study concerning the Adoption *Contact* Register, as if the researchers had made a mistake in including it.

Particularly strongly expressed were feelings where the adopted person was the relative's own child and where a wish registered by the adopted person not to have contact would prevent access even to basic information as to his or her well-being. Ironically, and very sadly, one of the reasons why some birth relatives would accept the introduction of a non-contact register would be that encountering it would at least tell them that their adopted relative was still alive at the time of registering the wish not to be contacted. This would, though, be a most convoluted means of ascertaining information which could be much less traumatically conveyed, with other non-disclosing information, by an adoption agency or other third party. This would require only a clarification of, rather than a change in, current policy.

> '*A veto – should include information, such as photos and letters, etc. Emotional damage could result with absolutely* No *reason given*.' (Female sibling)

Another reason for conceding what might be called the "negative acceptability" of a non-contact registration (i.e. a factor making it less unacceptable than the alternative) was that it would at least stop any further distressing speculation as to whether contact would ever be possible:

> '*Although a veto may be painful to encounter, it is perhaps preferable to the void, to not knowing what the relative thinks or feels*.' (Male sibling)

It might be considered that neither of these unacceptable alternatives need be the option considered by legislators or policy makers, since the information that the adopted person did not want contact could be conveyed in a potentially much less hurtful or even harmful way by a third party (see below). A third party approach might also be a better alternative in cases where the adopted person might need some assistance to talk matters through with his or her adoptive parents. Haimes and Timms (1985) found that the desire of adopted people to seek information about their origins was perfectly natural, but that fear of upsetting or appearing to betray the adopters was sometimes experienced as an obstacle. This was echoed by the following respondent who counted herself as "uncertain" about the proposal of a non-contact provision:

> '. . . *young people can be pressurised into blocking "for the family's sake".*' (Female sibling)

"Non-contact" mechanism for birth relatives

Just over a third of respondents (34.6 per cent, 588 people) felt birth relatives should have the right to register a wish not to be contacted, whilst an almost identical number (34.55 per cent, 587 people) thought they should not. This was the most evenly balanced "yes/no" response in the entire questionnaire and does not, therefore, represent a huge groundswell of opinion, or even a majority backing, for the proposed change. Of equal interest are the remaining third or so (30.8 per cent, 524 people) who did not know one way or the other. This degree of uncertainty, together with the evenly spread replies of the others, and the recurring confusion in the detailed comments about what was actually being asked, perhaps indicate that it is precipitate to introduce the non-contact idea into legislation when it has yet to sink into the public consciousness – even a public as interested in the topic of adoption contact as this one. Furthermore, more people went to the trouble of writing negative comments than positive ones, even though the question was posed in positive terms and without accompanying comment in one direction or the other. Once again, 159 people (16.1 per cent) felt a non-contact register would contradict the essential *raison d'être* of the Register and 285 people (28.8 per cent) stressed the relative's right of access to information.

Several key arguments related both to non-contact registrations for adopted people and to those for birth relatives. For example, 90 people in respect of an adopted person's position and 60 people in respect of a birth relative's, offered the unsolicited view that a registered wish not to be contacted should only ever be possible, if at all, through an intermediary. It was felt that no one should ever encounter one in a letter or by any other mechanism which did not involve direct emotional support. Post-adoption agencies in this country which offer a tracing service, and which were contacted as part of this research, could see the person originally registering the wish not to be contacted as gaining benefit, too, from the intermediary or third party. They have found that people whose initial reaction is to refuse a contact approach outright, when supported at their own pace to consider the idea that someone does want to contact them and offered ways in which this might be manageable for them, quite often change their minds. (For instance, personal communication with Birthlink in Edinburgh indicates that a majority of birth parents who have made a "no contact" registration decide to proceed to contact after all, once they know it is available.) Mixed feelings are, after all, the norm in this field of work. Questionnaire respondents, too, could envisage a change of heart taking place, since "no contact" decisions would be based on what the person imagined might result rather than on what the other party actually intended or could offer:

> '*In difficult circumstances a veto acts as a buffer to unwanted contact from certain quarters. Use of an intermediary seems to me better than an "iron curtain" veto, as it gives the opportunity for possible misunderstanding to be dispelled.*' (Male sibling)

Once again, this is an issue which overlaps with the question of whether a register is not best run as a service which has an integrated personal support and counselling service within it.

The comments against the introduction of a block on contact are numerous and strongly felt. Some relate to mistaken motives and others to unforeseen impacts. For example, some respondents dismissed the idea of non-contact registrations because they would prevent people, both adopted people and their relatives, from coming to terms with the past and finding out the truth. This may be hard to do, but blocking it out is not seen as the answer since the past really can disrupt the present, at a subconscious level, whereas fears of an actual person doing this are often illusory:

'*Truthfulness is a state to aspire to and essential for true psychological and physiological health, growth and development. Even the truly reluctant seem to find the catharsis of contact beneficial.*' (Birth mother)

'*Nobody should be able to deny the existence of another person, no matter how painful.*' (Birth mother)

'*Despite the protestations that the new life,* après *the adoption, could be damaged or destroyed by revelation, the reality is almost certainly different.*' (Birth mother)

There are also the powerful arguments, firstly, of the painful and damaging aspect of coming across a "non-contact" registration (the "slap in the face" argument) and, secondly, of the total lack of guarantees when one is in place that it will actually prevent contact being made (the "you can get round it anyway" argument). The force of the latter is that people would think that they had obtained – indeed, paid for – a safeguard when, in fact, there is no such thing. Both points are backed by comments in this study and also by actual experience overseas:

'*Finding a block would be like a slap in the face. If someone is absolutely determined to find a relative, there are other ways and means.*' (Birth mother)

'*Determined people can disregard it – it can simply be another way of raising revenue for governments. Vetoes seem to cause much more pain than a qualified rejection through an intermediary.*' (Birth mother living overseas)

'*It is used in Australia at present and it causes a lot of unnecessary anguish. Both sides should have the opportunity of representing their case to each other. Vetoes prevent this.*' (Birth mother living overseas)

The intermediary suggestion can also be perceived in two of the above comments. Those working in the post-adoption field have similar reservations to those expressed by individual respondents to the questionnaire. They also emphasise the shifting nature of feelings, viewpoints and events in adoption (the "too final" argument). Doreen Ward, of the

Natural Parents' Network, said in a telephone interview that she disagreed with registered blocks on contact, particularly in the form proposed in the draft Bill, because:

> 'I'm not sure if they serve a particularly useful purpose. The New Zealand experience has shown a veto does not stop people. I'm not sure of the purpose a veto serves unless it is to protect somebody from something which is impossible to handle. In most cases the situation is not as impossible as people think it is going to be. An intermediary service can act as a temporary veto and can provide an explanation. Circumstances in adoption change and you have to leave space for that change to occur.'

The then After Adoption – Post Adoption Services in Manchester also felt that a non-contact registration would not stop someone if they desperately needed to find their relative. The representative of the Post-Adoption Centre in London 'would hope [there] would be good use of intermediaries and the availability of counselling so you could make an informed choice'. The then After Adoption – Yorkshire and Humberside also expressed some concern over the finality of a decision to place a block on contact since:

> 'People do have ups and downs and do change their minds and might make a decision about that at one point in their lives that feels right and then something changes. Also, I feel until someone knows someone is wanting contact, they don't actually know how they will feel about it and to stop the possibility of that knowledge before it happens is difficult for me.'

There were also reflections on this mutability of feelings from individual respondents to the survey:

> '*Circumstances and feelings change in life and an absolute, irreversible veto may be regretted at some future point.*'
> (Birth father)

> '*I am anxious that a veto could be regarded as a final act, with no chance of lifting it should the person's attitude change with time.*'
> (Birth mother)

Non-contact registrations were seen by many as not only highly undesirable, but also unnecessary. At the end of the day, some respondents considered that there were already enough safeguards within the system of the Adoption Contact Register and that any further measures would therefore be inappropriate:

'*As the Register does not at present put people in touch unless they are both registered, why should anyone need a veto to protect them from unwanted approaches?*' (Birth mother)

'*An adopted person already has control over being contacted.*' (Birth mother)

'*The most effective veto is not to register!*' (Male sibling)

'*We are thinking here of vetoing freedom. The present system seems especially sensible. Both sides have choice.*' (Birth father)

The interest groups contacted as part of the present research were particularly struck by the fact that the "non-contact" proposals appeared to be the only significant change the draft Bill suggested in the entire post-adoption field, despite the fact that considerable discussion, together with policy and practice uncertainty over recent years (resulting in notoriously uneven treatment of people seeking contact in different parts of the country), pointed towards the need for the stance on post-adoption contact to be regularised in line with current social attitudes and up-to-date research findings. The inclusion in the Bill of only this one, essentially negative, change (a measure to allow people to say they did *not* want to do something), and of nothing positive, cast a pall over the whole document and was said to have already led to some retrograde movement in adoption agencies which had previously been incrementally introducing more enlightened practices, with good results. The present study highlights the same paradox:

'*It is only in recent years the laws are opening up for us . . . if a veto was allowed then that would be unfair again.*' (Birth mother)

2. Improvements suggested by birth relatives

There are two sources of data on suggested improvements arising from the questionnaires completed by relatives. The first is contained within the responses to a direct question on the subject, and the second consists of material gleaned from the responses overall, to the entire questionnaire.

When asked directly what changes to the Register they could suggest, three out of ten respondents (29.9 per cent, 383 people) did not feel that any changes were needed, or could not think of any in response to that form of questioning. Two in every ten (19.1 per cent, 244 people), however, wanted to see a more proactive approach to the release of information to relatives. Other popular suggestions – all, by now, familiar – included the provision of an intermediary and counselling service (13.2 per cent, 169 people, with a further 18 people suggesting a letterbox service between adopted people and birth relatives), increased publicity (15.2 per cent, 194 people) and some type of regular feedback from ONS, even if it was just to inform relatives that their details were still on the Register (18.5 per cent, 236 people). Thirty-five people (2.7 per cent) harked back to the question of fees and other charges and mentioned here the desirability of a cheaper service.

These suggestions were reinforced by detailed comments. Those

Figure 6
Suggestions for improvements to the Register

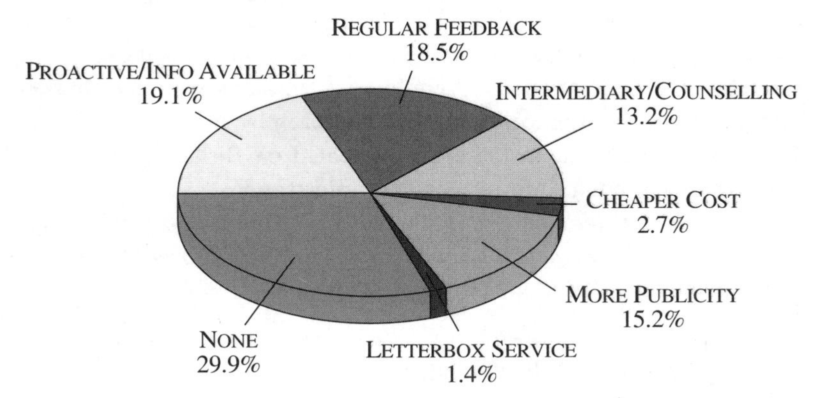

which follow, for example, reveal the intensity of feeling amongst birth relatives about the lack of feedback from the ONS once registration has been completed. Once again, they state the wish to have:

> '*A regular update on the situation, whether positive or negative. At the moment, it seems rather vague and most things seem rather unclear.*' (Birth mother)

> '*A note now and then to let you know if there's any news or not. A short personal letter helps. A friendly voice at the other end of the phone instead of the cold, impersonal person I spoke to.*' (Female sibling)

Other comments reinforced the conclusion that the publicity for the Adoption Contact Register is not as extensive as it might be. A male sibling suggested there could be a nationally advertised "adopted persons' contact week" where opportunities were provided for both parties to obtain literature about the Register and to make enquiries. Birth parents, too, wanted comprehensive, up-beat publicity:

> '*I think all adopted children should be given an information pack when they reach 18.*' (Birth father)

> '*Positive publicity – most media coverage of adoption reunions is extremely negative. It always focuses on the failures and disappointments.*' (Birth mother)

Several people suggested there could be a place for ONS to offer some sort of letterbox facility as part of the service accompanying the Register, whereby letters of introduction could be filed along with registration forms and passed on in the event of an approach by an adopted relative. This would be similar to the space allocated on Birthlink's (Scottish Register) registration form for personal information.

> '*If I could register a letter and it could be kept on files, I feel it would be warmer, a more human introduction. I sort of feel overwhelmed by the bureaucracy of it all.*' (Birth mother)

> '*The facility to hold copies of letters they might wish to leave on file if a match is made.*' (Birth mother)

'*Facility for filing any letters to the adopted person from relatives, in the event of a "match", to be passed with names and addresses. These may well create a better atmosphere for contact and possible dialogue.*' (Birth mother)

'*It would be wonderful to be able to send information on to my son after he has received my name and address. It may be too hard for him to take the huge step to contact. If he could be notified that I wished to send information, it may make contact easier.*' (Birth mother)

In addition, there was a desire for those involved in running the Adoption Contact Register to act, themselves, as intermediaries and to pass on to the adopted person the information that a birth relative had actually registered and wished to attempt contact. Interestingly, this is what the Children's Society has begun to do (Feast and Smith, 1993, p.34), as a step forward from leaving letters on file in case of a "linked" contact from the adult adopted person; the latter came to be seen as unsatisfactory, partly as a result of feedback from adopted people themselves who said they would have preferred to have been given the option of deciding whether or not to have the letter sent on. Feast and Smith concluded that, just because an adult adopted person has not sought their birth records information, does not mean they are not interested in their origins; there may be all sorts of reasons why they have not followed this up and most of those contacted by the Children's Society have found it a positive experience.

In the present study, several birth relatives made an articulate case for an intermediary service. They believed that hearing a relative had registered might constitute an appropriate stimulus to encourage an adopted person to take the somewhat daunting step of registering themselves:

'*When someone registers, couldn't a letter be sent to inform the opposite party that this has been done? It might make them register or at least give the matter some thought. To wait in vain hope of them thinking about it is soul destroying. At least you would know what you are up against.*' (Birth mother)

'*[The Register should have] the ability to pass on letters to adopted relatives to inform them of willingness/desire for contact.*' (Birth mother)

'*I think they should try and contact him [adopted person] and ask if he would like to be put in touch with me. If he then refuses that would be an end to the matter and I need never know his address. But at least he would have been put in the picture and could make his own mind up.*' (Female sibling)

'*I think OPCS [now ONS] could do a little more, i.e. they should be able to trace your lost one for you, then ask both sides if they wish to meet or not, which at least it would put you out of your misery.*' (Birth mother)

'*Perhaps if the birth mother registers then the adopted child concerned should be told and vice versa. I think then that it wouldn't be such a hit and miss affair.*' (Birth mother)

Those who suggested that counselling should be available made points such as the following:

'*Counselling offers time to reflect on confused emotions and to plan future courses of action.*' (Birth mother)

'*Emotional stability is not a foregone conclusion in an intact family. Therefore an adoption situation is even more difficult.*' (Birth father)

Certainly, many respondents' comments throughout the questionnaires reflected their surprise at how intense their emotions were in relation to registration and/or its aftermath.

Detailed changes proposed at the point of the link

The most popular suggestions for changes at the point of a link, from respondents overall, included, yet again, the introduction of a counselling and support service (21.2 per cent, 247 people) and allowing birth relatives to receive full details of their adopted relative (14.2 per cent, 166 people) – as the adopted person does about the birth relative – with an additional 48 (4.1 per cent) suggesting non-disclosing information at this point. Thirty-three people (2.8 per cent) proposed an intermediary, 18 (1.5 per cent) mentioned the desirability of follow-up from the ONS, and ten (0.9 per cent) wanted a letterbox service. A considerable number (1,262 people) did not propose any change, many because they could not envisage the precise process involved in a link. Some of the reasons given for proposing counselling included:

> '*Counselling would be helpful at this point. I would be on pins all the time, wondering if he was watching and waiting or, worse, speaking to me without making himself known.*' (Birth mother)

> '*The relative should at this point be offered the services of a counsellor experienced in matters of adoption, rather than having to seek out this help for themselves, which they are probably not be in a fit state to do at this point.*' (Birth mother)

The above point is an important one. At a time of such emotional turmoil, it would take great reserves of strength for individuals to seek out appropriate support or counselling for themselves, whereas, if such facilities were automatically available to those who wanted them, and there was official recognition of their value, they would be more easily accessible without additional difficulty for people who are already in an uncertain and vulnerable position.

Many of the birth relatives who had actually had a link offered suggestions for improvements to the process, which gives probably the best insight into the procedure and its limitations. Their proposals tended to arise from their greater knowledge of the emotional impact of achieving a link. Some people felt, for example, that they had lost control of the situation and that it had all happened too fast, without adequate time to prepare emotionally:

> '*I would like to be a little more in control of the process. This whole process has taken a number of years. I make the moves when I feel I can handle them.*' (Birth mother)

> '*You need a settling-in period before writing to the adopted person – maybe two weeks.*' (Birth mother)

Other suggestions were similar to those above: intermediaries, support and letterbox services, equal rights to information. Were initial contact to be carried out through an intermediary, for example, both parties could have a breathing space and time to adjust to the new situation:

> '*First contact should be made through a third party, so that the relative has some notice and chance to prepare themselves.*' (Female sibling)

Personal support or counselling was also proposed, to help cope with the practicalities as well as the emotions involved in a link:

> '*I had no idea what the next move might be. I phoned OPCS [now ONS] who were polite but totally unhelpful! Perhaps they could have a helpline with someone trained to support people in these situations.*' (Birth mother)

A further proposal was the facility to pass on some sort of letter to the adopted person at the point of the link, so that there could be an introduction prior to actual contact:

'. . . *hold a letter from relatives to be sent with the information. This may include the reason, background information and hopes for the future and family which we have now, so they can make a more informed choice about meeting their family or not.*' (Birth mother)

'*Perhaps it would be possible to provide an intermediary service so that I could have sent a letter to my daughter – I really felt at the time I wanted her to know how welcome she was.*' (Birth mother)

One birth mother recognised the difficulty for an adopted person who was given all the responsibility to make the next move once they had received details of their birth relative. Her reason for also sending details to birth relatives was so that they might share the initiative:

> '*If a match is made then obviously the adoptee is looking for contact too. The details they give should be sent to the registered birth relative as a mutual exchange of information. The initial letter of contact is hard to send and an adoptee may get cold feet, whereas a birth relative is likely to have maturity on their side to enable them to handle making the first move much easier.*' (Birth mother)

To sum up the general feeling of those birth relatives who had had a link, they would have liked the whole process to be more closely monitored by experienced post-adoption workers and for it to be recognised that:

> '*After contact is the critical time. The contact is only the beginning of a long journey for relative and adopted person.*' (Birth mother)

> '*I think this service should be personalised and conducted only by people experienced in post-adoption situations. In my experience, many people including social workers, have a naïve view of what being a "natural" mother really means.*' (Birth mother)

3. Potential changes suggested by the questionnaire

The questionnaire posed some specific questions related to possible increases in rights, both for adopted people and their relatives, in terms of facilities the Register might offer. These arose from consultation with post-adoption organisations and some therefore relate to quite specific situations which they have encountered in their day-to-day practice. It was a useful opportunity to gauge the responses of birth relatives to these.

Proxy for incapacitated adult adopted people

An overwhelming majority of relatives (86.3 per cent, 1,527 people) approved of the idea of a suggested provision, whereby an adoptive parent or other proxy could place an adopted adult's details onto the Register, in the event that they were too sick or incapacitated to do so for themselves, in order to keep open the lines of communication. Only 48 people were against this and the others were unsure or did not reply. In the absence of this provision (i.e. currently), a birth relative seeking an adopted person who is incapable of registering simply hears nothing and is left to imagine that this is because the adopted person has no interest in them, or that they may be dead. Although closed adoption is sometimes thought of as protection for the interests of adopters, there are, in fact, many adopters who (mindful, perhaps, of the success of increasing openness in adoption practice) would in fact welcome contact with the birth family of the person they adopted. Where the adopted person is capable of making their own decision this is, of course, a matter for them, but, where they are not, it seems harsh that the adopters are blocked from doing what they may sincerely feel is in the adopted person's best interests, or from extending the generosity of openness to the birth relatives. This category of "incapacitated" adopted people would include some with terminal illnesses or coma – where this could be the last chance of an exchange of information, or a reunion if desired by birth relative and adopters, before the adopted person died. It would also cover forms of disability requiring personal assistance or other help which the birth relative might be happy to offer from time to time, perhaps providing some respite for the adopters. Whatever the circumstances, the degree of support for this proposal would suggest that it could be introduced into legislation, as soon as an opportunity presented itself, without arousing controversy – particularly since it would only involve contact with any birth relative who had also chosen to register. It is, incidentally, a service which Birthlink in Scotland already offers (personal communication), having taken the view that an already socially disadvantaged group of people should not be disadvantaged further.

Information in the event of a death

There is a related question as to whether adoptive parents should be given the opportunity to place on the Register information about an adopted person who has died, either for the simple purpose of passing this information on to any birth relative who might be seeking a link, or to initiate contact with the birth family, if desired. This is not currently possible since Part I of the Register is open only to adopted people for initial registrations.

An overwhelming majority of respondents to this survey certainly did want to be informed if the adopted person died so, once again, this would be an uncontroversial measure. It is good news to learn that Southport will now, if asked to do so, record on any existing entry in the Register the information that the person concerned has subsequently died. This means that, in the event of a match between entries in the two parts of the Register, one party can be told that, sadly, the other has died. Otherwise, a birth relative would simply hear nothing further and would be left to assume that contact was no longer wanted by the adopted person. The new practice of annotating the Register entry still leaves unresolved, however, the question of contact being initiated between the birth family and the adoptive family of a deceased person, where desired. It is also only of assistance in cases where the information about a death is communicated to ONS. There is no provision for cross-referencing between the Adoption Register and other information held by the Registrar General who, of course, is notified of all deaths.

Birthlink in Scotland does allow registrations by adoptive parents where the adopted person has died and considers this an important service both to them and to birth relatives (personal communication). Without it, birth relatives are permanently deprived of information, are unable to face the finality of the situation and to grieve, and cannot seek contact with the adoptive family. The agency has reported a particular need for information amongst people who were involved in private placements since, in such cases, there would be no adoption agency to act as an alternative source of information about a death.

Right for under-age adopted people's details to be placed on the Register

More than twice as many people (54.3 per cent, 962 people) agreed than disagreed (25.4 per cent, 450 people) that adoptive parents should be able to place details on the Register for an adopted person who had yet to reach the age of 18, while one in five (20.4 per cent, 361 people) was undecided or unwilling to give a blanket response in one direction or the other. Clearly, this is a more radical proposal than the preceding one (although again, Birthlink in Scotland already provides such a service) but it nevertheless attracted considerable support. Once more, it would have no effect on any birth relative – or, indeed, any adoptive family – who did not choose to register their details. Given current adoption practice, adoptive parents would be advised to talk the matter through thoroughly with the adopted person before registering his or her details, and a typical scenario would probably be one where they were acting on behalf of a teenage adopted person who themselves actively wanted a link but was, as yet, too young to register (or on behalf of an incapacitated young adopted person, as above).

Right for under-age birth relatives' details to be placed on the Register
Once again, over half the respondents (51.9 per cent, 918 people) felt there should be the opportunity for those birth relatives who were under 18 years of age to place their own details on the Register. Ratios remained broadly similar to those responding to the previous question, with 26.9 per cent (475 people) giving a negative response to this suggestion and 21.3 per cent (376 people) uncertain how they felt about it. This option would, for example, allow young siblings of adopted people to make themselves available for contact. The particular needs of siblings have been little discussed in previous work and have emerged from this study as being of interest in their own right (see Chapter 9).

Conclusion
The one change proposed by Government during 1996, in a draft statute which otherwise completely ignored the rapidly changing world of post-adoption practice, was the "non-contact register". In the present research this notion gave rise to considerable confusion and produced no clear mandate for the change on the part of relatives.

Arguments which would need to be carefully considered before such a measure were to be introduced included the fact that it could give rise to a false sense of security in that it could be circumvented, and that it could be damaging for someone to encounter a block on contact, particularly if no intermediary were involved. In practice, organisations in the post-adoption field tended to report that those expressing the wish not to be contacted frequently changed their minds when they knew contact had become possible – yet the measure as proposed would allow no scope for such a change of heart. "Non-contact" registrations were, in any case, felt to be unnecessary in that no one is contacted through the Register who has not placed their name on it, and it is already possible for an individual to request that their name subsequently be removed.

Relatives' own suggestions for change were all in the opposite direction, towards the Register becoming more proactive and offering them greater rights to information, contact, intermediary services and searching. Lower fees, increased publicity and the need for an optional counselling service all resurfaced at this point.

The questionnaire itself posed questions about specific extensions to the Register service which could be contemplated. There was strong support for the idea of allowing the adoptive parent or other proxy of an incapacitated adult adopted person to place that person's details on the Register, and for information to be passed on in the event of a death. Smaller majorities also favoured allowing the names of under-age adopted people to be registered by their adoptive parents, and allowing under-age birth relatives, such as siblings, to register their own names.

The feeling from relatives, then, was that there was considerable scope for *positive* changes in the Register. There would appear to be a strong argument for the official discourse to turn in this direction.

Postscript

The current Government proposals in the draft Adoption Bill for a "non-contact" register appear to rest on an unresearched concern that some adopted people fear the unannounced re-entry of their birth families into their lives. This stereotype of intrusion is quite contrary to the tone which permeates the current study, where concern for the adopted person's well-being, and a desire to know whether contact would be welcome, predominate.

It is ironic that just when British research is emerging which backs the case for birth relatives to have greater rights (to rectify the damaging history of closed adoption), Department of Health spokespeople are implying that the birth relatives' case is well known and that what we lack is knowledge about adopted people's views about contact with their birth relatives. The background literature review underpinning this project revisited the work by John Triseliotis and by Erica Haimes and Noël Timms which established beyond doubt that adopted people have a natural desire to know about their origins. It also reviewed work which showed that reunions are predominantly positive and that success rates can be further increased by careful pacing and by providing support throughout the process.

It is not the case that birth relatives' views are yet well known in this country; still less that they have set the pace of change. Rather, the natural desires of birth relatives still go largely unmet and, as a group, they still feel unheard.

8 Relatives' views on openness in adoption

It seemed important to ask this sample of people, all of whom have been affected by a closed adoption, for their views on more open options in adoption. The following questions were therefore concerned with the degree of contact respondents would have preferred to have had with their own adopted relative in the past.

Contact in general

Well over half (58 per cent, 1,002 people) would have liked to have had some sort of contact between their own and the adoptive family. Over a quarter, 489 people (28.3 per cent), were not sure where they stood on this issue and 13.8 per cent (238 people) were opposed.

Contact prior to adoption

Though fewer replied in the affirmative, once again over half (54.9 per cent, 852 people) would have liked to have had some sort of contact with the adoptive family prior to the adoption actually occurring. Precisely as with the previous question, 489 people (which this time equals 32.4 per cent since fewer people replied overall) were not sure about this type of contact, while a smaller number, 198 (12.7 per cent), were opposed.

Contact during childhood

Slightly fewer again, but still approaching half of those replying (45.2 per cent, 704 people), would have liked contact during the adopted person's childhood, while slightly more than with the other questions were unsure about contact during this period (546 people, 35.1 per cent). Slightly more (307, 19.7 per cent), too, were opposed. This type of contact is therefore the most controversial, though still not particularly so. It must also be remembered that this is a biased sample. Closed adoption was all they had known and, at the time of the adoption with which they were concerned, birth relatives were clearly told that anonymity would be best for the child. It might be difficult now for them to question this (or to face a possibility denied to them), so that practice experience and other research findings might be better sources of guidance.

Contact post-18

Respondents were much clearer about the desirability of contact after the age of 18, which is understandable as this is the type of contact many were themselves seeking. Three out of four (74.1 per cent, 1,152 people) agreed with this, while 23 per cent (357 people) were not sure about it. The hesitation of this latter group may be because the type of contact and the method by which it was to be obtained were not specified in the question, or may reflect the persistence of mixed feelings, even after registration, or the fact that some people wanted information rather than direct contact. Forty-five people (2.9 per cent) said they were opposed, perhaps because the question did not specify any safeguards for the adopted person such as the use of an intermediary, or because contact as such was not what the respondent wanted.

Summarising the above four sections, it is safe to say that a clear majority of respondents backs all forms of contact between birth and adoptive families, with the least concern expressed about those forms of contact which do not involve the adopted person personally during childhood.

Additional questions were asked about more specific rights of access to information for birth relatives.

Right of birth relatives to apply for identifying information about the adopted person

Over half of the sample (58 per cent, 1,024 people) would like to have had access to the same level of identifying information as their adopted relation was potentially able to obtain about them. They saw this as enabling them to take a more proactive approach to seeking their relative, should they so wish. The qualitative comments overall reinforce the strength of this widely felt desire for more information, with siblings' views amongst the strongest (see Chapter 9).

Although those responding positively represent a majority – and over 1,000 people – at 58 per cent, there is clearly an element of caution in this result. For many (807 people, 55.5 per cent of all those responding to a follow-up question seeking detailed reasons), this was because they feared that contact they initiated might be too intrusive. This includes 90 people (5.7 per cent) who even wondered whether the adopted person had been told he or she was adopted, which could mean that the advent of a birth relative upon the scene would come as a particular shock. This was one of many points in the questionnaire at which the suggestion of an intermediary arose, in other words, someone to make an acceptable first approach to the adopted person and pave the way for reunion with the relative, if welcome. There were 261 people (16.5 per cent) who volunteered this proposal at this point. A bolder group of 702 people (44.5 per cent of respondents to this question) considered that what they believed should be their equal right to information was justified by the strength of their need for it, or the urgency of the information they wanted to convey (about the adoption or about a medical matter), or by the maturity of the parties involved.

On a general note, a birth mother highlighted the helplessness felt by many birth relatives because of the lack of information which is obtainable concerning the welfare of the adopted person:

'*It is inhumane to force these parents to continue to live their lives in torture, not knowing whether their child is involved whenever they hear of a major disaster – any one of the thousands of disasters over the years where there are reports of the death of a male/female of the same age as their son/daughter.*' (Birth mother)

Views on access to identifying information about adopted people

Birth relatives are far from insensitive when it comes to the issue of accessing identifying information. Almost a third of the sample, 32 per cent (505 people), felt that it would be too intrusive to make a contact themselves and a further 16.5 per cent would only do so through a third party, to ensure that as little upset as possible occurred. However, 35 per cent (552 people) argued that they just wanted to have the information.

The following quotes illustrate the fact that many birth relatives simply require basic information to set their minds at rest:

'*I would be more settled if I knew definitely if he was all right. It's worse than if someone died – to know they are out there and you can't contact them.*' (Birth mother)

'*She is my flesh and blood and the need to know is very strong.*' (Birth mother)

'. . . *to have got news of her progress would have made it easier for me, I think.*' (Birth mother)

There is an awareness of the need for caution and discretion in order to avoid unnecessary upset for the adopted relative and indeed, some birth parents are still of the opinion that they have no right to contact, however strong their own needs:

'*It is very tempting to want to track my adopted son down but he has a right to remain private, until he is ready to be contacted.*' (Birth mother)

'*I do not think after having the baby adopted, I have a right to turn her world and her parents' world upside down, just because I am older and wiser and more able to be a mother.*' (Birth mother)

'*It doesn't seem ethical or fair. His choice needs to be made by him and those who know and love him. I have no right to meddle as I am a virtual stranger.*' (Birth mother)

'*My heart says "yes", [for access to information] but my head says it should be the prerogative of the adopted person to do so.*' (Birth mother)

Despite the above reservations, a majority of birth relatives were in favour of an increase in their rights to information about adopted relatives, with a general feeling that times have changed and laws need to reflect these changing attitudes and circumstances:

'*The law says that all mothers of adopted children must go to their grave never knowing what became of their child; the secrecy surrounding adoption is wrong.*' (Grandmother)

'*England is still tied down with a medieval way of thinking and secretive orders from the court to hide everything.*' (Birth mother)

'*In New Zealand when an adopted person reaches 20, the birth mother may obtain details to trace the adoptee. I am unable to do this because of the archaic laws in the UK. It is frustrating and unnecessarily painful – I have always had to be passive and wait, and I cannot be active in this most fundamental part of my life.*' (Birth mother living overseas)

Most people, then, supported the idea of access to disclosing information for birth relatives, either with safeguards (such as the use of intermediaries) to protect adopted relatives from unwanted contact, or simply on the basis that adopted people are now adult and would be able to deal with any approach from a birth relative and make their own decisions regarding the advisability of taking the contact further. Either way, the pro-disclosure argument is founded on the belief that adopted adults have the right to know that a birth relative wishes to contact them.

'*Birth parents should have the same rights as adopted adults to information that may lead to contact. However, I believe that contact is best made via a trained intermediary and also specialist counselling should be available.*' (Birth mother)

'*I feel that I should have the same rights in this respect as adopted people; since my daughter is now 30, I feel she can no longer be considered a child who needs protecting from her past. I would use an intermediary in any case.*' (Birth mother)

'*Providing that there are safeguards for the adopted person to prevent unwanted intrusion, I would welcome some mechanism which would enable me to advise the adopted person that her original family is interested in contacting her.*' (Female cousin)

'*I think once the adopted person has reached 18 then the natural mother, if she wishes, should be allowed to know where to contact. The worst that can happen is they refuse contact, but at least the adopted person would know contact is wanted.*' (Birth mother)

> '*We are both adult human beings and it is a particularly bad start that I am unable to show my concern for my son by contacting him.*' (Birth mother)

Finally, one birth mother who gave up her child for adoption many years ago, raised the fact that, since the law had changed access to information for adopted people, increased rights for birth relatives should also follow:

> '*They [adopted relatives] can apply for information at 18 years, even though older birth relatives were promised they would never be told. So I think it's only fair that it works both ways.*' (Birth mother)

This is arguably the biggest gap in the present system and the one which should be most carefully thought about.

Conclusion

Around half the birth relatives who responded to this survey would have liked to have had contact with the adoptive family before placement and during the adopted person's childhood. Three-quarters had no reservations about contact post-18. Almost three people in five – over 1,000 people – considered that birth relatives should have the same rights of access to identifying information as adult adopted people, with some proposing an intermediary as a safeguard. There was a general feeling that times have changed and that secrecy is both outmoded and damaging.

Postscript

Although granting such rights to birth relatives would represent a major revision to current legislation in England and Wales, that legislation itself represents an artificial and relatively recent imposition of assumptions grounded in dismissive or punitive attitudes towards birth mothers and a lack of recognition that other birth relatives might want to be involved. Altering the law in favour of birth relatives would represent no more fundamental a change than happened in relation to adult adopted people in the Children Act 1975, since that Act overturned a situation in which birth relatives thought they could never be traced. It has been overwhelmingly successful in operation, as has legislation overseas which has accorded rights to birth relatives and also post-adoption contact services operating on behalf of relatives in this country.

The argument currently being voiced within the Department of Health – that birth relatives have no grounds to ask for greater rights because they are no longer related in law to the adopted people with whom they seek contact – bears no more weight than would an argument in the opposite direction maintaining that, because adult adopted people are not legally related to their birth relatives, they therefore have no right to seek information about their origins. Law, policy and practice in England and Wales now live comfortably with the availability of access to birth records for adult adopted people and no one is suggesting turning back the clock on that initiative. Furthermore, if birth relatives have no foundation of relationship, why is incest still recognised between them and the adopted people to whom they were formerly related. And why was Part II of the Register created? Above all, why do many birth relatives experience such overwhelming reactions to legislation which they perceive as blocking their aspirations to re-establish contact? Clearly, a legal severance of ties does not end the social and emotional connections which people feel and it is the reality of these which the research findings presented here, once again, challenge us to acknowledge.

9 New thoughts on "other relatives"

As was revealed in Chapter 1, there is a dearth of literature on relatives other than the birth mothers of adopted people. From the present study, some new thinking about siblings has emerged which would benefit from further work, together with a further reflection that birth fathers need to be conceptualised differently from birth mothers since they have had, and continue to have, a different experience.

Siblings' viewpoints

The qualitative material in this study has highlighted the fact that there is a case for focusing on the viewpoint of siblings of adopted people as a separate and unique group of birth relatives with their own interests and feelings which need to be addressed. This has not happened to date in other research. There were 347 sibling respondents, or 19.6 per cent of the sample overall. On Part II of the Register as a whole, at the cut-off date of 30 September 1995, siblings constituted at least 9.8 per cent and possibly as high as 20.3 per cent of the total. They are therefore considerably over-represented in this research, making it a still more useful opportunity to obtain their views. In fact, it seems that virtually all the siblings on the Register may have taken part in the research, perhaps because they have never been consulted before and/or because they have fewer emotional obstacles to participation than birth parents.

Although "sibling" is an unattractive word with an air of jargon about it, it has been used here as a shorthand to cover all varieties of full- and half-brothers and sisters (i.e. those sharing one or both parents), as well as brothers- and sisters-in-law. (The phrase "brothers and sisters", on the contrary, might have seemed to imply only those of the full blood.) Even the fiancé of a birth sister, whose current status would not give him the right to place his name on the Register, spoke movingly during the

Table 10
Age of siblings

Age	n	%
>29	37	10.8
30–39	90	26.2
40–49	85	24.7
50–59	92	26.7
60<	40	11.6
Totals	344	100.0
Missing data (non-responses)	3	–

meeting with the Council for Equal Rights under Adoption for Siblings (CERAFS), one of the interest groups interviewed for the research, about the loss to him of a future brother-in-law who would not be able to attend his and his fiancée's wedding or be part of their life as a married couple.

The 347 siblings in the survey encompassed the whole age span, distributed as shown in Table 10. They were particularly evenly spread, and heavily concentrated, in the 30 to 60 age range (with surprisingly few under 30). Despite this spread across age groups, their perspectives reflected common themes whether they were young or old, and whether they had always known they had an adopted sibling or had only recently learnt of his or her existence (sometimes, for older respondents, on reading family papers following a death). In fact, a quarter of siblings described the trigger factor for placing details on the Register as being the recent discovery of the existence of the adopted person, and they were the predominant group of birth relatives who made any mention of this happening. (This is self-evident, in fact, since birth mothers know by definition that they have had a child, and there were only small numbers of any other category of relatives in the study.)

Siblings across the board felt they had been deprived of an essential ingredient in their lives:

'*I felt that I did not belong to anyone and always felt that something was missing.*' (Female sibling)

'*There is always this missing piece in your life that you are anxious to fill.*' (Female sibling)

They considered this a particular kind of loss, special to them, which is frequently overlooked because attention is paid to birth parents, not to other relatives. Siblings felt a special kind of neglect of their perceptions and interests:

'*Usually it's the parent–child relationship that gets focused on.*' (Female sibling)

'*. . . there are no laws or thoughts for a person in my situation. You've either got to be the adopted person or the natural parent.*' (Female sibling)

The birth sibling experience may involve searching for a person the sibling has never met, even fleetingly as a baby – who has, in fact, never had a physical presence for them:

'*People overlook the loss to other siblings living with a "ghost".*' (Female sibling)

Despite this – and the source of these feelings would repay further research – siblings clearly felt they had lost the closeness of a natural relative.

Another reason siblings felt they were in a different position from birth parents, was that they had played no part in the relinquishment of their sister or brother. In many cases, they had not been old enough at the time to be aware of the situation (or not yet born), and they certainly had not been consulted. However, they considered the adopted person as a part of their family and a part of themselves, and they were deeply grieved at the loss of that person in their lives. This added an urgency to the frustration or anger they expressed at their current lack of rights to make direct contact:

'*I was deprived of my brother – I never had the chance of laughter and tears that a brother and sister should share. I have waited long enough – the barriers should be dropped.*' (Female sibling)

Similar issues arose about the use of third parties, to help balance the interests of all those involved, and about the need for a counselling service as were raised by respondents more broadly. With siblings, however, these matters were typically couched within a strongly expressed desire for direct access to information and/or contact:

> '*We both have families we don't know anything about, and we should both have the same choice of information which should be done through a third party*.' (Male sibling)
>
> '*I think I should have had counselling as I wanted more than anything to belong to someone and so my desire to find her strengthened for the wrong reasons*.' (Female sibling)

The orientation adopted by siblings, and the kind of language they use, tends to be a discourse, not only about strongly experienced feelings and needs, but also about "rights" which are being denied by a current legal process and/or by past events which lay quite outside their own sphere of influence. On both counts, they experience the situation as inherently unjust. Their language is less often tempered by the mixed feelings many birth mothers express. For example, birth mothers write not only about their needs but about their own "guilt", whether or not they consider there is any good reason to feel guilty. (The simple fact that this was a dominant ethos surrounding the need to place a child for adoption is probably still influencing their emotional reaction to the situation.) Birth mothers often expend great care in their comments, too, on balancing their own needs against those of their adopted "child" and they are more likely to use "rights" language in relation to the adopted person's right, now, to go about their own life and to make their own choices whether to instigate a reunion process, rather than about any rights they might perceive themselves as having. Of course, birth relatives of all degrees of relationship, including siblings, do write about this balancing of rights:

> '*The adoption register is a way of giving the adopted person the choice of contact. I wouldn't be happy invading his life if he was happy and had no desire to find us*.' (Female sibling)
>
> '*I feel I have no right to find her unless she wants to be found this way. I'm here waiting should she want to contact me*.' (Aunt)

But some siblings are able to write in a sharper, more unidimensional way. They tend to believe that the authorities should recognise their particular position and give rights to access information, either to all birth relatives or particularly focusing on those cases where it is a sibling who is wishing to reunite with their brother or sister:

> '*I think, as a sister, I should have the right to find her. I think certain rights should be given to siblings.*' (Female sibling)

> '*I was disgusted to learn that I had no legal way or right to find him.*' (Male sibling)

Often, it is not that siblings are neglecting to think about the situation from the surmised point of view of the adopted person, but more that, being broadly of the same generation, there is no question for them of thinking in terms of protecting the interests of a child. They were not involved in the adoptive placement of a child – so do not have the situation cast in that adult/child perspective – and nor are they now, of course, thinking about contacting someone who is a child. It is an entirely adult/adult matter in personal and social terms, but they feel that the law does not reflect this, that it is outmoded and over-protective:

> '*The adoption laws are out of date and, now my brother is 56 years old, it seems archaic that we are still not mature enough to be given information which could lead to relief of frustration and some contact. My pain and his pain are ignored, as brick walls preventing two-way information seem to be everywhere.*' (Female sibling)

> '*These laws should be changed for certain people. They should be interviewed and feelings and circumstances like age should be taken into account. I have gone 50 years without a sister.*' (Female sibling)

> '*It is not the Government's right to deny me (or anyone else) the right to know my sisters. If we have difficulty dealing with meeting them, let us work that out for ourselves.*' (Male sibling living overseas)

This line of reasoning leads to the suggestion of a proactive approach being made to the now adult adopted person, on behalf of the birth relative seeking contact, so that he or she could determine what should happen:

> '*I think they should try and contact him [brother] and ask if he would*

> *like to be put in touch with me. If he then refuses that would be an end to the matter and I need never know his address, but at least he would have been put in the picture and could make his own mind up.*' (Female sibling)

Siblings are, then, using a language concerned with an inappropriate denial of what they see as inalienable rights. Feelings run high when they consider the loss of many years of contact as a result of sociolegal intervention:

> '*The powers that be destroyed 48 to 49 years of our lives, through no fault of ours. We were just babies when our mother died at the age of 21, then [we were] parted. Was this fair?*' (Male sibling)

The nascent pressure group for siblings, CERAFS (Council for Equal Rights under Adoption Law for Siblings), based in Inverness, wishes to see a change in the law giving siblings the right to have an approach made on their behalf by the placing agency (where one was involved) to the adoptive parents of an adopted person aged between 18 and 24, or direct at age 25 and above. CERAFS has described siblings as 'innocent parties separated for life' (in a letter to the social work press), thus emphasising that any adoption decision will have been made by an older generation and that siblings will not have been consulted and will not have had any control over the outcome. The organisation is also dissatisfied with the geographical variation in attitudes between, and services offered by, adoption agencies (including social services and social work departments). The Secretary of CERAFS feels that the fact of adoption, the stance of one adoption agency and the current state of the legislation have deprived her of her brother. She cannot even send him a birthday card as the agency which placed her brother will not pass it on. She considers that the Adoption Contact Register is a blocking system – it is shackled by the constraints of the present adoption law. This essentially negative view implies that the Register is where many relatives come to a full stop and even, perhaps, that the post-adoption situation might actually develop towards greater openness if the Register did not exist at all, enshrining as it does one fixed position on what limits should be placed on relatives seeking contact.

There is something of a "raw edge" to views expressed by siblings. Their anger and pain are unalloyed by feelings of guilt or by the ethos that surrounded the child care decision-making of the past. One aspect perhaps to be wary of in this position is that it can tend to hold connotations of siblings being "blameless" and birth parents being "blameworthy". Whilst it is certainly fruitful to pursue the line of thought that both siblings and their adopted brothers and sisters (by whatever degree of blood or marriage) are still being denied whatever would have flowed to them in personal or social terms from the knowledge and experience of being related to one another – in what now appears an unjust way – it would not seem any more fair to take action to give them rights to the exclusion of other birth relatives. And there is no reason why this need be the case since, although different categories of relative may phrase their argument somewhat differently or propose different courses of action, they are similarly motivated by a need for more information and could all be encompassed by the same safeguards built into any new legal framework. This point will be returned to in the discussion section below.

Siblings who are adopted people themselves

A proportion of siblings are themselves adopted people. (Unfortunately, this issue was not identified by the researchers in time to incorporate a question which would have identified the number of adopted siblings who participated in the current study.) This will typically have arisen where one birth parent or one family group – for reasons of death, ill-health, births outside marriage, or difficulties in social functioning – has placed for adoption, or has faced the removal of, more than one child and the children have, often over time, gone into different adoptive families.

A sibling who is also an adopted person can provide a unique insight into the situation faced by adopted adults as they consider the decision whether to place their details on a contact register or to follow up a link:

> '*I feel often an adoptee lacks the self-esteem to make contact. The fear of rejection is very great.*' (Female sibling)

In other words, adopted siblings can articulate the mixture of feelings which may inhibit adopted people from seeking contact even when, in other ways, they may strongly desire it. Adopted siblings can also highlight the particular irony of the fact that they have absolute rights, as adopted people, to information over which they lack any rights in their other capacity as birth relatives. The imbalance in the law, in the way it attempts to treat differently what it regards as two distinct categories of people, is placed in stark relief when the two different treatments affect the same person. In practice, this means that any quest an adopted sibling launches to find his or her birth family, after pursuing the legal right to obtain birth records details, will hit a total obstacle if another member of that birth family is also adopted – an obstacle which other adopted people do not encounter:

> '*Why should I be denied my birth sister's details when I was adopted myself?*' (Female sibling)

For those siblings who are themselves adopted people there is a further complication, referred to earlier, in the process of placing details on the Register. To all intents and purposes, a sibling who is also adopted should have their details placed on both Parts I and II of the Adoption Contact Register, in order to ensure that they cover all options for contact, but the Register's literature does not adequately explain this cross-over of identities. Nor does ONS currently have the discretion to operate any adjusted charges to cover the additional expense involved in such a situation.

Birth fathers

There were only 68 birth fathers in the study, which was not unexpected since their representation is lower than that of birth mothers in all post-adoption contexts. There were 157 fathers on Part II of the Register at the cut-off date for the research, who may include step-fathers. They constitute 4.6 per cent of relatives registered, and 3.8 per cent of respondents to the questionnaire. In other words, fathers are slightly under-represented in this study, but the margin is small. There has not, to date, been an opportunity to analyse separately the responses of birth fathers, although this may occur in the context of a later stage of the work.

The responses of birth fathers in suggesting changes to the present Register system highlight two aspects of fathers' situation which sets them apart from other groups. Both relate to their relative invisibility, a factor which they tend to share with fathers generally in the child care arena (O'Hagan, 1997) and which is now seen as caused by an interplay between, on the one hand, the fact that some men welcome the opportunity to absent themselves from family matters or from situations where they will be considered to be at fault, and, on the other, the tendency of professionals to look more to women where children are concerned. In the context of the present study, these tendencies are compounded by the fact that so many babies placed for adoption in the past were born outside marriage and were seen by most people at the time (including, presumably, a proportion of birth fathers) as the mother's responsibility.

Two birth fathers who participated in the current study remarked that they felt their position was somewhat isolated and posed difficulties of its own which merited special attention. One complained about what he felt was the general lack of support in the post-adoption field for men in his position; he considered that:

'*The weakness of all the help groups was, they were very much geared to mothers, not fathers*.' (Birth father)

The second raised the question of proof of identity, which the researchers also heard about from ONS staff; birth fathers are the group who involve the most paperwork because they can find it the hardest to prove their relationship to the adopted person, whatever the extent of their care or involvement at the time of the birth or since. This birth father asked:

'*Please help birth fathers whose names do not appear on birth certificates, to be recognised. Register is too sexist! Possibly a sworn affidavit and change in the law would help us men.*' (Birth father)

ONS staff were not unaware of the complications for birth fathers and stressed that they provide considerable assistance to fathers during the process of gathering together the evidence required to satisfy the Registrar General as to their relationship to an adopted person (personal communication with Adoptions Section).

Conclusion

There is more work that could be done in analysing the existing data from the perspectives of birth relatives other than birth mothers and, clearly, far more research that could be undertaken. One of the present authors has commenced a further study of the siblings in the sample reported here, involving in-depth telephone interviews with about 40 people. This would also be a fruitful field of enquiry for other researchers and also for monitoring of work by practitioners and policy makers. There is no doubt that birth relatives more widely are making an increasing call upon post-adoption services and that this will have implications both for resources and for refining our understanding of their particular experiences and viewpoints.

10 A comparison between the contact registers available in Great Britain

As the issues of personal support, intermediary services, letterboxes, and so on have been identified as important elements in the process of a birth relative coming to terms with, and adapting to the possibility of, contact of some sort with an adopted relative, it is worth comparing the different approaches of the two contact registers currently in operation in England and Wales, and the one in Scotland. (A new one is just being established in Northern Ireland.) There is, in fact, a continuum of models in existence, from the Adoption Contact Register's administrative style – backed only by a list of appropriate counselling organisations and leaving it up to an individual to contact these if they feel the need to do so, either for a third party service or to receive more general help – to the contact register run by NORCAP (the National Organisation for Counselling Adoptees and Parents) where each step of every link is carefully paced and supported. Further differences relate to the level of fee charged and the statutory or voluntary nature of the organisation running the particular register.

Statutory/voluntary status and fees or charges

Firstly, the ONS Register has a statutory base, having been established under, and working to a remit set out in, child care legislation covering the whole of England and Wales, and it is staffed by civil servants. It charges a registration fee to cover the administrative costs incurred, which is significantly higher for birth relatives, at £27.50, than for adopted people who are charged only £9.50. This difference is justified on the grounds that the existence of a relationship with an adopted person, as well as that individual's own identity, must be verified in the case of a birth relative, so that there is more work involved. Unfortunately for the relative, the actual cost to them has tended to be much higher, not uncommonly in the region of £100 (with one agency reporting a case of £180 being spent), as they have been required to provide original copies of all relevant certificates (e.g. of birth and marriage) to prove their identity, that of the adopted person and their relationship to one another, and they have had to pay a fee for the issue of these if not already in possession of them.

Secondly, NORCAP is a voluntary agency, registered as a charity, with a national catchment area. It was established and is run by people with a personal involvement in adoption who believe strongly in rights to contact but also in the need for a careful support structure, provided by people with a close knowledge of what is personally and emotionally involved. It has a fee structure but keeps charges as low as possible. There is a £5 registration fee to place details on the register. In addition, if a relative wishes to become a member of the organisation, this costs £15 in the first year and £12.50 thereafter. Membership allows access to a quarterly magazine which provides a medium of communication between people involved in the contact process. NORCAP's register is longer established and larger than the Adoption Contact Register. It had its first link in 1986 and is running at about three times the number of links achieved by the official Register (though at approximately the same rate as a percentage of registrations). NORCAP not only operates a register but also offers advice on searching, an intermediary service in reunions, a non-disclosure contacting service operated through adoption agencies on behalf of birth parents (where the adopted person is aged at least 25), and general support in relation to post-adoption concerns. It has built up considerable experience in all matters relating to post-adoption contact.

Finally, Birthlink is run by Family Care in Edinburgh, a voluntary agency with charitable status whose wider functions are those of an approved adoption society, and employs professionally qualified staff. Birthlink is the national register for Scotland. It is funded by monies received from the Scottish Office and subscribing local authorities, as well as by donations from adopted people, birth parents and relatives, and has no fee for registration though donations are welcome. All of its funders and users would be seen as needing to be consulted were the present funding arrangements to become unviable without contemplating a fee. Optional membership of Family Care is available at an annual cost of £10 (£2 unwaged) and affords voting and representation rights, together with a flow of information through annual reports and newsletters. Birthlink operates to a model of social work expertise and is able to call upon the adoption counsellors located within its parent agency.

Perhaps the difference in staffing between the three registers – the civil servant, adoption participant and professional social work emphases – explains many of the other variations between them.

Model of operating

The procedures followed, once a link has been made between the details of a birth relative and an adopted person, are very different between the three registers and can be visualised as points on a continuum. The ONS Register sends the name and address of the birth relative to the adopted person; the birth relative is only informed that his or her particulars have been passed on. From that point onwards, it is entirely at the discretion of the adopted person whether to take contact any further. There is no inclusive counselling for either person involved but, as mentioned previously, some organisations' addresses are included in the explanatory booklet (ACR 110) and ONS staff also suggest the use of counselling services to telephone callers who appear distressed. The booklet further explains the facility for a birth relative to use a contact address other than their own or that of a third party, if this would be easier or otherwise beneficial for the individual concerned.

The Birthlink Register adopts the middle position in the continuum. Professional support is an integral part of the service and is seen as an inseparable part of the issuing of information. Once a link has been identified, a social worker contacts both parties and the opportunity is provided to talk about the implications of the link. In addition, there is the possibility of including personal details on the initial registration form, such as present circumstances, family attitudes to registration, medical information or explanations about the adoption "decision", if people wish to do so. This can prepare the ground prior to a link occurring and means that an adopted person does not have to initiate contact from "cold", but has some information upon which to build a relationship. The operation of the Birthlink Register, and of Family Care's counselling and tracing services, is grounded in its long history as an adoption placement agency and its involvement in research, both of which have influenced the careful development of its practice.

NORCAP provides the most "guided" service, with intermediary assistance at all points of the process and with comprehensive counselling based on considerable experience of past reunions. Once a link is identified, a letter is sent to the relative saying information may be available about the person they are looking for, and they are asked to send a copy of the original birth certificate in order to confirm this documentation. Once this has been done, NORCAP acts as an intermediary between both parties. Initially, a letter is exchanged without any identifying details, and this is sent via NORCAP. Each party is informed by telephone of the imminent arrival of the letter. By the second or third letter, a photograph is normally included but each case is treated individually and flexibly. When telephone contact is requested, NORCAP will endeavour to arrange the first call, irrespective of the time of day. It is usually the adopted person who feels most comfortable with initiating the call, but, should their nerve fail, the organisation ensures that no one is left waiting without word for an indefinite period. At all stages of the linking process, NORCAP guides both parties and is there for support and advice, as and when it is required. Additionally, Christmas cards are sent to everyone who has achieved a link in any one year, allowing an opening for people to get back in touch if they feel the need to do so. Clearly this is a much more personal, individualised service than the official Adoption Contact Register was set up to be, and it works hard to take into account the varying needs of its users.

It may perhaps seem odd that the voluntary agencies are more interventive than the statutory one – when the resonances of the terms "statutory" and "voluntary" in wider child care practice would imply a weighting the other way round – but this stems from the fact that Birthlink and NORCAP work to a social work or counselling model, while the Adoption Contact Register operates to an administrative or "civil service" model. At the periphery of its work, the Register has developed a telephone response service to enquirers which, perforce, strays beyond administrative bounds, but this remains essentially *ad hoc*; it was never conceptualised as a personal support service and is unlikely to feature as such in any service development or staff training strategy.

The staff operating it have developed unwritten boundaries between the queries they attempt to answer in full themselves, and those they suggest to callers would be more appropriately referred on elsewhere – typically to agencies with a counselling or tracing function or to adoption agencies holding original records, backed by a social work service. This telephone work can be seen as inhabiting the grey area between the two purist models of register services – the supported, counselling model and the impersonal, administrative model – and it serves to illustrate, perhaps, that it is impossible to hold the latter model completely within impersonal bounds. The emotions of those who have lost touch with relatives through the adoption process are simply too strongly felt and sometimes too "messy" to be satisfied by initial postal contact followed by silence (as was also found in the process of conducting this research when quite a number of people sent letters with their questionnaires on a range of topics, including asking for advice or help with tracing, which the researchers dealt with by suggesting other sources of assistance).

Which is the preferred model?

The above account leaves wide open the question of what type of register service is to be preferred, especially in the light of the difference of views expressed by the research respondents. Some actually preferred a kind of clinical impersonality which did not intrude into their lives and were content with the service as currently offered from Southport. Certainly, there should be no lessening of standards of confidentiality, record-keeping or overall efficiency, whatever other changes may be made. Many others, however, revealed a preference for a personally supported service to be available, given the strength and complexity of the emotions involved in the whole matter of contact. This was also the thrust of criticism when the Register was first established (Hodgkins, 1989; BAAF, 1991).

The addition of the proposed "non-contact" measures to the official Register service in England and Wales will, of course, strain the administrative model still further. The notion of treating the placing of a block on contact as yet another bureaucratic measure is frankly bizarre. Such an action is usually a reaction to a maelstrom of emotion – and likely to cause another when it is encountered by the other party. Given that the argument in favour of support and counselling has already cropped up throughout this book in respect of the Register's service as it stands (which merely invites people to use it as one way of seeking contact that is positively desired on both sides – an apparently bland concept but actually seismic in reported emotional proportions), the idea that the present, non-supported model could encompass a further measure which would *positively invite people to place on record the opposite of the message the other party is desperately hoping to encounter,* with all the emotional aftermath that that would entail, might be argued to be negligent of a duty of care to the users of that service. There could certainly be resultant suicide attempts and other forms of self-harm and mental disturbance. The Adoptions Section staff at the now ONS might have their own views about what staff training or support they would require in order effectively to handle the telephone calls which would ensue from people encountering non-contact registrations.

At the very least, post-adoption specialists consider that no one should ever be informed in bald fashion that a wish not to be contacted has been registered. The very strong advice is that the person placing the block on contact should be encouraged to accompany it with a non-identifying letter explaining the reason and sharing some basic personal information. Given that assistance with writing such a letter is probably best located within a social work-style or supported service, it might be even better to engage the person in a process which could help to resolve some of their fears and which might make direct or inter-mediated contact possible after all. This research study has confirmed what practice wisdom already suggested: that there are not, in fact, two kinds of people – those who want contact and those who do not – but one continuum of people who hold in varying degrees of balance a personal need to make sense of the past, a desire for emotional stability in the present, typically a desire not to hurt other people with whom they have past or present connections, and a view that closed adoption has left a tangled legacy which we might see as the responsibility of the state to disentangle. The same person will very often occupy different points along the continuum as particular feelings and memories, life events and life stages, and wider social changes unfold. Any service which is set up to meet the needs of such people cannot expect to be fully successful if it operates in black and white terms, rather than in fluid shades of grey.

Are two Registers really necessary?

A further unanswered question is whether the nation needs two separate register services in England and Wales. Certainly, for any individual who is considering registering, it means that they must either pay twice or potentially miss a link on the other register. The NORCAP Register has been established longer and has more people on it. However, it appears to achieve a similar *percentage* rate of links as the Adoption Contact Register (see Figures 4 and 5). Since there is no way of knowing the number of individuals registered on both, it is impossible to say whether an amalgamation of the two would increase the likelihood of a link, or to what degree. NORCAP campaigned for the establishment of the Adoption Contact Register but, in the event, was dissatisfied with the model adopted and therefore continued to run its own system in parallel – in order to offer a more personally supportive service with a fuller information exchange.

The two registers could only now draw together if, either, the Registrar General was able to discharge his statutory duty by contracting out the maintenance of the official register to NORCAP or to an organisation whose operating model NORCAP approved of, or, if the official register altered its *modus operandi* to the extent that NORCAP felt able to disband its register and advise everyone on it to re-register at Southport. If such rationalisation were considered unnecessary or unworkable (even as a longer-term aim to follow a period of discussion and negotiation), there is a strong argument, in the light of the responses to this study, for the official register to establish a direct link with a counselling service (as Birthlink has done) – any call upon which would remain dependent on the preference of the individual concerned – and for an opportunity to be provided to record non-disclosing personal details on the registration form (again, along the lines of the Scottish model). As a spin-off from the Advisory Group meetings for this research study, staff of Birthlink and of the Adoption Contact Register have met to exchange ideas and this can only be to the good.

If a direct link between the Adoption Contact Register and a counselling service were to be considered, this could either be on a contractual basis to an agency like NORCAP (with appropriate funding support) or to the existing network of those providing birth records counselling. The problem with the latter would be that it would become entangled with the varying levels of priority, training and attention accorded to post-adoption services around the country and would almost certainly lead to a very uneven provision. Just as the Register itself operates as a specialist and skilled operation, within its current remit, it has the right to expect a link with a focused and specialised counselling service, suitably knowledgeable about matters concerning birth relatives. One ex-local authority fostering and adoption officer, now working in a post-adoption agency, remarked at the Post-Adoption Forum conference in September 1996 that she had known very little about birth parents until she changed her job, and that she had had to learn a very great deal thereafter. This does not bode well for giving any new responsibilities for counselling relatives to local authorities as one of the key providers.

Continuing support for a Register?

At another level, until the wider question of increased rights for birth relatives is resolved, any register service will continue to have to deal with strong emotions of frustration and anger which do not relate directly to its own work. In other words, there is an extent to which registers with no contacting or tracing service act largely to mop up negative feelings about "the system" and its denial of rights to relatives of adopted people. Post-adoption activists report, too, that adoption agencies sometimes "fob people off" by telling them about the Adoption Contact Register instead of offering help with tracing or passing on non-identifying information.

This situation has caused some of those who originally campaigned for the establishment of the Register to question whether its arrival has done more harm than good, especially since the number of links actually achieved has been relatively small. On balance, however, post-adoption workers interviewed as part of this research all still came down in favour of the Register's existence but welcomed this independent review as an opportunity to rethink its purpose and manner of operation.

11 Conclusion

The findings of this study logically lead to a call for the process of reviewing and amending adoption law now to extend to a complete reconsideration of statute and guidance in respect of birth relatives' access to non-disclosing and disclosing information, tracing services, and third party and direct approaches to adult adopted people, as well as of the opportunities for birth relatives to pass on disclosing and non-disclosing information about themselves. The law has not, in this sphere, kept pace with changing social attitudes or behaviours, and adoption and post-adoption agencies have been left completely uncertain as to what level of service equates with good practice. As a result, while some agencies continue to close the door on birth relatives or to offer less than is wanted, others offer a full-scale service for which they have not been adequately resourced, doing so at least partly on the moral grounds that post-adoption work involves meeting present need caused by past socio-legal practice that was founded on assumptions which everyone in this field now considers to be out of date and damaging.

Nor does it appear particularly logical to conceptualise any future direction of change in terms of "protecting" a group of adults – adopted people – that has no equivalent in other areas of law and no basis in research findings about their wishes. Naturally, a barrier of secrecy which the state imposed, the state should think carefully about removing – just as it did when giving adopted people access to birth records which had the capacity to lead them back to birth mothers who were living under the impression that their identity had been permanently concealed. In the case of birth relatives, the equivalent safeguard could be to release information through an agency which would act as a third party in any proposed contact with the adopted person, so that the adopted person could clearly express a wish not to have contact, where this applied, or could fully discuss the manner and timing of contact where desired. And although there has been much talk of the desirability of counselling services in this book, these are advocated entirely on a voluntary and self-regulated basis, integral to any new structure which might be devised. The imposition of counselling, and its use to control people's eventual access to information, has given rise to great controversy elsewhere, in parts of Australia for example, and is not supported by the findings of this research. Thus the third party is not proposed as a "back door" route to counselling.

Meanwhile, the release of non-disclosing information to (and about) birth relatives appears to be entirely uncontentious and a regularisation of policy on this could be introduced straight away. This would, in itself, relieve a great deal of the pain and distress which birth mothers, in particular, describe at not knowing even whether their child is alive or dead.

Any rethinking should also take on board the needs of those who are unable to call on the full range of existing services. Some people, for example, lack the necessary information to make an entry on the Register. They include adult adopted people who were abandoned at birth and, on the relatives' side, those like the birth mother who wrote to the researchers because she had been too young and too distressed at the time of her confinement even to keep a note of the date of her baby's birth. For others, the Register may be virtually all they have. Adoptions which were not arranged through an agency, for example, leave those concerned unable to access agency records or support services – as also happens to those who are denied help by an agency with a rigidly narrow policy.

Though they may tend to argue their case somewhat differently from one another, the two largest groups represented in this study, birth mothers and siblings, both wrote with some force about the damage and distress closed adoption had caused in their lives, its outmodedness and its irrelevance in adult/adult situations. They were by no means without sensitivity to the interests of the adopted person – often, indeed, putting these before their own – but considered that it was not beyond the bounds of possibility to devise a system of safeguards which could provide a safe framework around a more proactive service.

Since this study was conducted, adoption has been much in the news as a result of one high profile reunion, speculation about future legislation and associated political speeches. The findings of this research indicate that the use of adoption in an earlier era to "solve" social problems has left a considerable aftermath of pain and distress and that, even now, the extent of openness which is desirable in adoption and post-adoption situations remains unresolved. The courage and generosity of the respondents to this survey, in sharing their experiences and their views, would be best rewarded by the devotion of public and political time and attention to considering what adoption has meant in the past to those most affected by it, and what it should mean in the future.

Appendix I
Research on the Adoption Contact Register – a summary

This project involved a self-selected sample of those birth relatives of adopted people who had placed their details on Part II of the Adoption Contact Register. The Register was established under the Children Act 1989. It is the responsibility of the Registrar General and is administered by the Office for National Statistics (ONS, formerly OPCS) in Southport. Everyone who registered on Part II between the starting date of the Register's operation, 1 May 1991, and the research cut-off date, 30 September 1995 (a total of 3,404 people) was asked if they would be willing to complete a questionnaire to give their experiences of the working of the Register and their wider views on post-adoption services. Sixty-nine per cent (2,346) agreed to participate in the survey and, subsequently, 76 per cent of these (1,784 people or 52 per cent of Part II registrations as a whole) returned the completed questionnaire. This included 314 people living overseas. This was considered an excellent response rate for a postal survey and added weight to the findings of the research.

Some interesting details about participants

Of the 1,784 birth relatives who completed the questionnaire, there were many more women than men (1,571 women or 88 per cent of the total). The majority of respondents were birth mothers (71.9 per cent) and the second largest group was made up of 347 brothers and sisters of adopted people (19.6 per cent). In addition, 68 birth fathers took part, 33 aunts and uncles, 32 grandparents and 18 other relatives. The most typical person was a birth mother in middle years, hoping that contact could be re-established with an adopted person who was now a young adult. Over 200 relatives, however, were over 60 years of age and were hoping to make contact before they died. Siblings ranged most widely in age. Nearly 100 people had only recently discovered the existence of an adopted brother or sister, sometimes on reading family papers after a death. Seventy-two people in the sample had had the desired "link" with the adopted person – a higher proportion than on the Register as a whole, where there is currently roughly a 3 in 100 chance of a link.

Main results

Publicity

The research revealed a deficiency in publicity for the Register. Only 45 people had seen the poster advertising it. Nearly a third of the sample had heard about the Register through the media, and nearly a quarter from adoption agencies and social services. Most people felt there should be widescale, regularly repeated official publicity, together with a drive to have the issue picked up more widely, for example, in a soap opera storyline. Publicity overseas and UK publicity in languages other than English also need to be thought about. There is only a tiny number of black people on the Register at present. A higher profile would attract more adopted people and relatives to register, thus increasing the rate of links, and would reassure others that the service is still active. On the other hand, it would seem wise to consider other aspects of the findings reported on here, and any desirable changes, before undertaking a major publicity drive. Also, given that the name of the Register is misleading – because it does not exist to make contact, merely to record details in the hope of a link – any future publicity would need to make very clear exactly what was being offered.

Reactions to the Register

Three quarters of the sample had felt positive when registering, particularly at the official recognition of birth relatives as a group (in contrast with the adoption practice of the past) and the opportunity to take an active step. There were some mixed feelings, too, about where registering might lead, and growing frustration from those who had heard nothing. The information booklet was generally welcomed, although some thought a more user-friendly presentation would be preferable, together with a simpler way of finding out how to apply.

Fees

Relatives pay £27.50 to register, almost three times as much as adopted people, because there is more administration involved in checking their details – and despite the fact that they have fewer rights in the event of a link because they can only wait for the adopted person to decide whether to contact them. Although more than twice as many people thought the fee was fair as thought it was unfair, there were a good many negative comments. These ranged from the injustice of ruling out contact for people who could not afford registration, to the view that imposing a fee was like continuing to punish birth mothers. Some felt that adopted people should pay little or nothing so that more would register; others that no one should pay since the state was effectively putting right its own mistakes of the past. Since the research only included people who had been able to pay the fee, it cannot say how many people have been deterred. One in five had thought twice because of the cost, though.

General views on the service received

The high standard of efficiency and confidentiality maintained by the staff at Southport was appreciated. On the other hand, some people found the predominantly bureaucratic approach somewhat impersonal, and ill-suited to the inevitably emotional nature of trying to achieve post-adoption contact (which, for many people, also brings back memories of giving up the child). In connection with this, one of the recurrent themes throughout the research was the need for personal support. A large majority of people, 82.5 per cent (1,451 people) would like to see optional counselling provided as an integral part of the service. This point was raised by post-adoption organisations when the Register was first established but the answer given then – that people would be able to register under the address of a post-adoption agency and use its support in the event of a link – has not worked very well. Only 240 people in the sample had used this opportunity and fewer than half the respondents were aware that there was a list of support organisations printed in the introductory booklet they had been sent. Three-fifths had lacked support while deciding whether to register. Several people wrote about the processes both of going on the Register and of having a link as being far more emotional than they had imagined. Some would have appreciated help in knowing what to expect from a link and in pacing it more slowly. Over three-quarters of the sample as a whole thought that support would be helpful in the event of a link. Those who were still waiting also described heightened emotions: a quarter of the sample described being on the Register as a negative or frustrating experience. Over 300 people preferred the wider range of services offered by other organisations (such as intermediaries, information exchange and tracing) and almost half the sample had tried other methods of seeking contact. The telephone calls which are dealt with in Southport are sometimes from distressed, anxious or angry people who might well benefit from direct access to experienced post-adoption workers, as might those who mistakenly think the Adoption Contact Register can help them search for the adopted person. Both the NORCAP and the Birthlink (Scottish) registers operate a more "guided" or "supported" model.

In whose interests?

Many aspects of the questionnaire brought out the extent to which birth relatives were thinking of the adopted person's interests, as much as and sometimes more than their own. Although a majority hoped above all for a reunion, seven out of ten people had also thought that their own registration would be in the adopted person's interests. One in 12 was not thinking of their own interests at all, while many others thought that everyone concerned would benefit from contact. And this was borne out by the finding that the majority of those who had had a link had, indeed, found it positive.

Desired outcomes

There was a great need to give and receive information: to obtain the most basic details about the adopted person's current well-being and what kind of person they had become; to tell them that they were loved, what their birth relatives were like and, for birth mothers, why they were placed for adoption. Some people had medical information to convey. The vast majority of people wanted every kind of contact: 88.5 per cent wanted information; 85.6 per cent wanted an exchange of letters and photographs; 74.8 per cent hoped to talk on the telephone; 87.3 per cent desired a meeting; 76.8 per cent would have liked an ongoing relationship; and 77.7 per cent wanted to be told if the adopted person had died. Twenty-one people particularly wanted to thank the adoptive parents. Sadly, however, only one in five believed they would actually see the adopted person again, while twice as many felt certain they would not.

Although three-fifths of the sample did express a positive view about the existence of the Register, it clearly is not meeting their full needs or desires in its present form. A majority of people considered that a move to sharing non-disclosing information would be uncontroversial for everyone. A smaller but often angry group considered that an active tracing and contact service should be available to birth relatives. Siblings, in particular, tended to talk in terms of the rights of adopted people, now adult, and of their brothers and sisters – who have been denied a relationship for many years through no fault of their own – to decide for themselves whether they now want contact.

"Veto" proposals

There was considerable confusion over the questions related to the proposed introduction of a "non-contact register" and almost a third of respondents were unsure of where they stood with regard to this issue. Although just over half agreed that adopted people should have the opportunity to express a desire not to be contacted, the chief concern was the right to choice – which some felt could equally well be safeguarded by an approach through an intermediary. There was no majority for a "non-contact" provision for birth relatives (who, once again, tended often to be putting other interests before their own). The detailed comments painted a picture of some concern and anger; experience overseas has shown that a block on contact can never be guaranteed to be effective, and it is very distressing for anyone who comes up against it. A number of respondents and post-adoption professionals also pointed out that any sort of "veto" is too final; it bears no relation to the flux of emotions to which thinking about contact gives rise. Here again, an intermediary may be better placed to help an individual think through all aspects of what contact might mean, for them and for other people, and to reach a decision with which they can feel comfortable. Certainly, given the criticisms, above, of a service unsupported by counselling, the introduction of blocks on contact without support, and without even an exchange of non-identifying information, would appear inhumane and potentially dangerous.

Rights for birth relatives

A majority of birth relatives in this study were not satisfied with the current extent of their rights to information. Non-disclosing information exchange was considered uncontroversial. Going further, 58 per cent (1,024 people) would have liked to have had equal rights to identifying details in the event of a link between themselves and an adopted relative. They considered that times had changed and that the law should reflect these changing circumstances. Half were also sure that they would have preferred an open adoption to a closed one. In addition, the following were all supported: rights for adoptive parents to be able to place details on behalf of an incapacitated adopted adult (86.3 per cent); adoptive parents to be able to place details for adopted people under 18 (54.3 per cent); and birth relatives who are under 18 years of age to be able to register (51.9 per cent).

Conclusion

The research study brought to light a number of proposals for positive changes in the working of the Adoption Contact Register. These will now be shared with the relevant authorities in the hope that they may influence law and practice.

Appendix II
Organisations providing advice and counselling to birth relatives of adopted people

If you would like to talk to someone in confidence, the organisations listed below provide counselling services. NORCAP and the Natural Parents' Network are national organisations. Alternatively, if there was a voluntary adoption society involved in an adoption with which you may be connected, they can be contacted for help and advice. All local authority social services and social work departments also provide advice on post-adoption matters.

NORCAP
112 Church Road
Wheatley
Oxfordshire
OX33 1LU
Tel: 01865 875000

Natural Parents' Network
c/o Sheila Walker
79 Crockford Park Road
Addlestone
Surrey KT15 2LN
Tel: 01932 828930

The Post Adoption Centre
5 Torriano Mews
Torriano Avenue
Kentish Town
London NW5 2RZ
Tel: 0171 284 0555

After Adoption – Manchester
12–14 Chapel Street
Salford
Manchester
M3 7NN
Tel: 0161 839 4930/4932

After Adoption – Yorkshire
Grove Villa
80–82 Cardigan Road
Headingley
Leeds LS6 3BJ
Tel: 0113 230 2100

For Hampshire residents only:
Hampshire County Council
Post Adoption Social Workers
Headquarters Family Placement Team
Trafalgar House, Trafalgar Street
Winchester SO23 8UQ
Tel: 01962 841841

West Midlands Post Adoption Service
92 Newcombe Road
Handsworth
Birmingham
B21 8DD
Tel: 0121 523 3343

After Adoption – Wales
Unit 1
Cowbridge Court
58–62 Cowbridge Road
West Cardiff CF5 5BS
Tel: 01222 575711

Birthlink
Family Care
21 Castle Street
Edinburgh EH2 3DN
Tel: 0131 225 6441

The Merseyside Adoption Centre
316–317 Coopers Building
Church Street
Liverpool
L1 3AA
0151 709 9122

For Nottinghamshire residents and those whose adoption was arranged in Nottinghamshire:
Support After Adoption
14 Strelley Road
Nottingham
NG8 3AP
Tel: 0115 980 4819/20

Appendix III

The questions asked in the questionnaire which was sent to respondents are reproduced below. Please note that what follows does not replicate the original layout and does not, for example, show the space that was allowed for answering open-ended questions.

A study of Relatives' Use of the Adoption Contact Register

We would like to ask you some questions about your experience of the Adoption Contact Register run by the Adoptions Section, Office of Population Censuses and Surveys (OPCS).

(If you wish to write more on particular questions, please feel free to include extra pages. Please state clearly which questions you are writing more about.)

1. How did you *first* hear about the Adoption Contact Register?
(please tick only one box)

National press ❑
(please give more details)

Local press ❑
(please give more details)

Word of mouth ❑

Magazines ❑

Adoption agency ❑

Don't know ❑

Television programme ❑
(please give more details)

Radio programme ❑
(please give more details)

Support group ❑
(please give more details)

Social services department ❑

Library ❑

Poster ❑

Other (please specify)

2. Did you see the original poster publicising the Adoption Contact Register?

Yes ☐ No ☐ Not sure ☐

If you answered yes, what did you think about it?

3. Do you think the Register is well enough publicised?

Yes ☐ No ☐ Don't know ☐

Where else could it be publicised?

4. Do you think the publicity should be repeated from time to time?

Yes ☐ No ☐ Don't know ☐

5. Currently, there is a registration fee to have details placed on the Register; relatives of adopted people are charged £27.50.

Do you think that the fee charged to put your name on the Register was fair?

Yes ☐ No ☐ Don't know ☐

Any comments?

6. Adopted people wishing to place their details on the Register are charged a fee of £9.50.

Should the fee be equal for both relatives and adopted people?

Yes ☐ No ☐ Don't know ☐

Any comments?

7. Did the level of the fee make you think twice about putting your name on the Register?

Yes ☐ No ☐ Don't know ☐

8. What was your first reaction to finding out about the Register?

9. When you first contacted OPCS they would have sent you the explanatory booklet *The Adoption Contact Register* (ACR110). Was the information contained in this booklet . . .

easy to understand ❑

reasonably understandable ❑

difficult to understand ❑

If you found it difficult to understand, could you please tell us what was difficult about it.

10. Did any of the following people help you to understand the Register? (please tick all that apply)

Adoptions Section (OPCS Southport)	❑	Support group	❑
Someone in social services	❑	A friend or relative	❑
Someone helped but I'm not sure who it was	❑	No one helped me	❑
Someone at adoption agency	❑	Post adoption centre	❑
Other (please specify)	❑		

11. Did any of the following people give you counselling or support during the period when you were deciding to place your name on the Register? (please tick all that apply)

Counselling service	❑	Adoptions Section (OPCS Southport)	❑
Someone in social services	❑	Friend or relative	❑
No one gave me counselling or support	❑	Support group	❑
Someone at adoption agency	❑	Post adoption centre	❑
Someone gave me counselling/ support but I'm not sure who	❑	Other (please specify)	❑

12. Have you used the service of a third party or intermediary who has provided an alternative address to be placed on the Adoption Contact Register on your behalf?

Yes ☐ No ☐

If you have answered Yes, which organisation acted as a third party or intermediary for you?

13. Were you aware that OPCS provides a list of organisations that are able to provide advice and counselling services, if required?

Yes ☐ No ☐ Don't know ☐

14. Do you think that counselling or support services should be made available as part of the OPCS service to relatives?

Yes ☐ No ☐ Don't know ☐

15. After first finding out about the Register, how long was it before you decided to write in?

Immediately ☐ Over 3 months ☐

Within a month ☐ More than a year ☐

1 to 3 months ☐ Don't remember ☐

16. Why did you decide to place your details on the Register?

17. Could you tell us if there were any particular triggers or circumstances in your life that influenced your decision to place your details on the Register?

18. When you placed your deteails on the Register what did you think or hope you would achieve by doing so?

19. For whose benefit did you place your details on the Register? (please tick all options that apply)

Yourself ☐ The adopted person ☐

Other relative ☐ Other (Please specify)

20. If an adult adopted person was unable, through incapacity or illness, to place their details on the Register, do you think an adoptive parent or other proxy should be able to do so on their behalf?

Yes ❑ No ❑ Not sure ❑

21. Should adoptive parents be able to place details on the Register on behalf of an adopted person who is under 18 years?

Yes ❑ No ❑ Not sure ❑

22. Do you think that relatives of adopted people, under the age of 18, should be able to place their details on the Register?

Yes ❑ No ❑ Not sure ❑

23. Was it learning about the Adoption Contact Register that first made you think that it might be possible to have contact with the adopted person or obtain information about them?

Yes ❑ No ❑ Not sure ❑

24. Do you think that you as a relative should be able to apply for information about the adopted person so that you could make contact yourself if you wanted to do so?

Yes ❑ No ❑ Not sure ❑

Could you explain why you think this way.

25. Which of the following would you like to be the eventual result of placing your details on the Register?
(please tick all the results that you would like).

Information about the adopted person ❑

Exchange of letters and/or photos with adopted person ❑

To talk to adopted person on the telephone ❑

A meeting with the adopted person ❑

An ongoing relationship including meetings ❑

Exchange of medical information ❑

To be informed in the event of the death of the adopted person ❑

Not certain at present ❑

Other (please tell us what this is)

26. There is a possibility that a measure could be introduced which would allow both a relative and an adopted person to place in the Register a block on being contacted (a veto).

Do you think this option of a veto should be available for use by an adopted person?

Should be available ❑

Uncertain if it should be available ❑

Should not be available ❑

Why do you think that?

27. Do you think this option of a veto should be available for use by a relative?

Should be available ❑

Uncertain if it should be available ❑

Should not be available ❑

Why do you think that?

28. How long have your details been placed on the Register?

Up to 6 months	❑	2 yrs to under 4 yrs	❑
Over 6 months but under 1 yr	❑	Over 4 yrs	❑
1 yr to under 2 yrs	❑	Don't know	❑

29. Have you been contacted by Adoptions Section (OPCS) to tell you that your adopted relative has also placed their details on the Register and so will have been sent your name and address?

Yes ❑ No ❑ Don't know ❑

If Yes, please tell us about this. Have you heard anything further, has this led to a meeting and how have you felt about what has happened?

30. Do you think that it is a good idea to have someone help a relative cope if the adopted person makes contact?

Yes ❑ No ❑ Don't know ❑

If you have answered yes or no, why do you feel this way?

31. Can you tell us what impact, if any, your involvement with the Register has had on your feelings or emotional state?

32. Can you think of any ways in which the service offered to relatives such as yourself (by Adoptions Section, OPCS) could be improved, from the point at which you are informed that your adopted relative has also placed details on the Register and will be sent your name and address?

33. Have you tried to make contact with the adopted person by other means?

Yes ❑ If Yes, go to question 34.

No ❑ If No, go to question 36.

34. Which of these methods did you use? (tick all that apply)

Your own enquiries ❑

Paying for a private investigation ❑

Another contact register ❑

A post adoption service (please specify)

Other support group (please specify)

Other (please specify)

35. If any of the above provide a service that was closer to what you required than the service provided by Adoptions Section, OPCS (under current adoption law), then please tell us how it was closer to your ideal?

36. Do you think that there should be some contact between birth family and adoptive family?

Yes ☐ No ☐ Not sure ☐

If No, go to Q. 40.

37. Should there be contact before adoption?

Yes ☐ No ☐ Not sure ☐

38. Should there be contact during childhood?

Yes ☐ No ☐ Not sure ☐

39. Should there be contact after the adopted person reaches 18?

Yes ☐ No ☐ Not sure ☐

40. When the adoption order was made did you ever expect to see the adopted person again?

Yes ☐ No ☐ Not sure ☐

41. What would you most like to know about the adopted person that you don't know at the moment?

42. What would you most like the adopted person to know about you that they do not know at the moment?
(Please do not reveal names or addresses or other information which could identify you).

43. As a relative of an adopted person, to what extent does the Register fulfil your needs and why?

44. Can you suggest any improvements to the Register?

45. What is your exact relationship to the adopted person

Birth mother ☐ Birth father ☐

Grandparent ☐ Brother or sister ☐

Other (please describe)

46. Are you related to the adopted person . . .

By blood ☐ By marriage ☐

47. Are you related to the adopted person . . .

On their father's side ☐ On their mother's side ☐

48. Was your adopted relative involved in a transracial placement?

Yes ☐ No ☐ Don't know ☐

49. Was the adoption placement made through an adoption agency?

Yes ☐ No ☐ Don't know ☐

50. Was the making of the adoption order contested in court?

Yes ☐ No ☐ Don't know ☐

Finally, we would like to obtain some details of yourself to provide a general picture of the people who have answered our questions. This is because the findings of research tend to be taken more seriously when the respondents can be shown to be typical of the wider population. All information will be treated in confidence and will not identify you.
(please tick the appropriate box)

51. Are you?

Male ☐ Female ☐

52. Within which of these age groups do you belong?

Under 20 years ❑ 40–49 years ❑

20–29 years ❑ 50–59 years ❑

30–39 years ❑ 60+ years ❑

53. Please tick your ethnic origin.

Black African ❑ Black Caribbean ❑ Black (other) ❑

White ❑ Indian ❑ Pakistani ❑

Bangladeshi ❑ Chinese ❑ Asian (other) ❑

Other (specify)

54. Do you live overseas?

Yes ❑ No ❑

If yes, which country do you live in?

55. Which region do you live in?

56. Are you currently in employment?

Yes ❑ No ❑

If you answered Yes, go to Q. 57.

If you answered No, go to Q. 58.

57. What is your occupation?

58. What was your last occupation?

59. What is the highest educational qualification you have?

Appendix IV

ADOPTED?

want to make

contact?

ARE YOU AN ADOPTED PERSON?

ARE YOU A RELATIVE OF SOMEONE WHO HAS BEEN ADOPTED?

ARE YOU OVER 18 YEARS OF AGE?

We may be able to help you. Please write to:

OPCS
The General Register Office
Adoptions Section
Smedley Hydro
Trafalgar Road · Southport PR8 2HH

For further copies write to: BAPS · Health Publications Unit · DSS Distribution Centre
Heywood Stores · Manchester Road · Heywood · Lancs OL10 2PZ

AD1

Appendix V

The questions used in the telephone monitoring exercise by the staff of the Adoptions Section of the OPCS at Southport are reproduced below. Please note that this does not replicate the original layout.

Phone Monitoring Sheet

Please record the following information about any telephone calls you deal with.

1. How long was the call?

Start time End time

Or total length of call (mins) ❑

2. Caller's sex? **Male** ❑ **Female** ❑

3. Caller's relatedness to adopted relative.

4. Please make an assessment of the emotional state of the caller.
(tick appropriate state(s) that apply)

Calm ❑ Not certain ❑

Distressed ❑ Other

5. Please make a brief summary of the reason for the telephone call.

6. Were you or a colleague in OPCS able to deal with the call yourself?

Yes ❑ No ❑

7. Did you have to refer the caller to someone else outside the OPCS?

Yes ❑ No ❑

If Yes, where was the caller referred to?

References

Adcock M, Kaniuk J and White R (eds.) (1993) *Exploring Openness in Adoption*, Significant Publications.

Argent H (ed.) (1988) *Keeping the Doors Open: A review of post-adoption services*, BAAF.

BBC '40 Minutes' series (1989) *Who'll Win Jeanette?*, British Broadcasting Corporation (television programme).

Bouchier P, Lambert L and Triseliotis J (1991) *Parting with a Child for Adoption: The mother's perspective*, BAAF.

British Agencies for Adoption and Fostering (1991) *The Adoption Contact Register, England and Wales*, Practice Note 20, BAAF.

British Agencies for Adoption and Fostering (1992) *Child from the past – Information for parents who placed a child for adoption years ago in England and Wales*, BAAF (leaflet).

Catholic Social Services (1985) *Open Adoption*, Catholic Social Services (video tape), New Zealand.

Clark B (1989) *My Search for Catherine Anne*, Lorrimer, Canada.

Cooper C (1993) 'A mother for life', *Community Care*, 4 February, pp 21–22.

Day C (1979) 'Access to birth records: General Register Office study', *Adoption & Fostering*, 98:4, pp 17–28.

Department of Health and Social Security (1976) *Access to Birth Records: Notes for counsellors*, DHSS (booklet).

Department of Health and Welsh Office (1996) *Adoption – A service for children; Adoption Bill – A consultative document*, Department of Health.

Department of Health, Welsh Office, Home Office and Lord Chancellor's Department (1993) *Adoption: The future*, HMSO (Cm 2288).

Department of Health Social Services Inspectorate (1995) *'Moving Goalposts': A study of post-adoption contact in the North of England*, Department of Health.

Deykin E Y, Patti P and Ryan J (1988) 'Fathers of adopted children: a study of the impact of child surrender on birthfathers', *American Journal of Orthopsychiatry*, 58:2, pp 240–248.

Dominick C (1988) *Early Contact in Adoption: Contact between birth mothers and adoptive parents at the time of and after the adoption*, Wellington, Research Section, Department of Social Welfare, New Zealand.

Feast J, Marwood M, Seabrook S, Warbur A and Webb L (eds.) (1994) *Preparing for Reunion: Adopted people, adoptive parents and birth parents tell their stories*, The Children's Society.

Feast J and Smith J (1993) 'Working on behalf of birth families – the Children's Society experience', *Adoption & Fostering*, 17:2, pp 33–40.

Field J (1991) 'Views of New Zealand birth mothers on search and reunion', in Mullender A, 1991b *op. cit.*

Fitsell A (1989) 'Relinquishing mothers share experiences', *Adoption & Fostering*, 13:4, pp 39–41.

Fratter J (1991) 'Adoptive parents and open adoption in the UK', in Mullender A, 1991b *op. cit.*

Garber R (1995) *Disclosure of Adoption Information*, Ministry of Community and Social Services, Government of Ontario, Canada.

Gediman J S and Brown L P (1989) *BirthBond: Reunions between birth parents and adoptees*, New Horizons Press, USA.

Grey E (1971) *A Survey of Adoption in Great Britain*, HMSO, Home Office Research Study No. 10.

Griffith K (1991a) 'Access to adoption records: the results of the changes in New Zealand law' in Mullender A 1991b, *op. cit.*

Griffith K C (1991b) *The Right to Know Who You Are: Reform of adoption law with honesty, openness and integrity*, Katherine W Kimbell (limited edition), Canada.

Griffith K C (1997) *New Zealand Adoption History and Practice, Social and Legal, 1840–1996*, Katherine W Kimbell, Canada.

Haimes E and Timms N (1985) *Adoption, Identity and Social Policy*, Gower.

Hall T (ed.), (1980) *Access to Birth Records: The impact of Section 26 of the Children Act 1975*, Association of British Adoption and Fostering Agencies.

Harrison C and Pavlovic A (1996) 'Working in partnership with lost parents' in Argent H (ed.) (1996) *See You Soon: Contact with children looked after by local authorities*, BAAF.

Hester M and Radford L (1996) *Domestic Violence and Child Contact Arrangements in England and Denmark*, Policy Press.

Hodgkins P (1989) 'Adoption Contact Register', *Adoption & Fostering*, 13:3, pp 3–4.

Howe D (1989) *The Post-Adoption Centre: First three years, Research Report No. 4: Birth Mothers*, University of East Anglia.

Howe D, Sawbridge P and Hinings D (1992) *Half a Million Women: Mothers who lose their children by adoption*, Penguin.

Hughes B (1996) 'Openness and contact in adoption: a child-centred perspective', *British Journal of Social Work*, 25:6, pp 729–747.

Inglis K (1984) *Living Mistakes: Mothers who consented to adoption*, George Allen & Unwin, Australia.

Iwanek M (1987) (A Study of Open Adoption Placements: The experiences over a period of time of 17 adoptive families and 14 birth mothers who had entered into an open adoptive agreement), Mary Iwanek, 14 Emerson Street, Petone, New Zealand.

Kaniuk J (1993) 'Openness in adoption: practice issues' in Adcock M *et al.*, *op. cit.*

Kosonen M (1996) 'Maintaining sibling relationships: neglected dimension in child care practice', *British Journal of Social Work*, 26:6, pp 809–822.

Lambert L, Borland M, Hill M and Triseliotis J (1992) 'Using contact registers in adoption searches', *Adoption & Fostering*, 16:1, pp 42–45.

Lancette J and McClure B A (1992) 'Birth mothers: grieving the loss of a dream', *Journal of Mental Health Counseling*, 14:1, pp 84–96.

Leeding A (1980) 'The local authority experience' in Hall T, *op. cit.*

Lindsay J W (1987) *Open Adoption: A caring option*, Morning Glory Press, USA.

Logan J (1996a) 'Birth mothers and their mental health: uncharted territory', *British Journal of Social Work*, 26:5, pp 609–625.

Logan J (1996b) *Post-Adoption Arrangements for Openness and Contact: An evaluation of an information exchange scheme,* University of Manchester, Department of Social Policy and Social Work.

Mallows M (1991) 'Transracial adoption – the most open adoption', in Mullender A, 1991b *op. cit.*

Millham S, Bullock R, Hosie K and Haak M (1986) *Lost in Care: The problem of maintaining links between children in care and their families*, Gower.

Mullender A (1991a) 'Adult adoption information in New Zealand: key differences from England and Wales', in Mullender A, 1991b *op. cit.*

Mullender A (1991b) *Open Adoption: The philosophy and the practice*, BAAF.

Mullender A (1991c) 'The spread of openness in New Zealand', in Mullender A, 1991b *op. cit.*

NORCAP (National Organisation for the Counselling of Adoptees and Parents) (1986) *Shared Experiences: A collection of stories from NORCAP NEWS 1 to 12*, NORCAP (No longer in print; new edition due in late 1997).

Office of Population Censuses and Surveys (1991) *The Adoption Contact Register: Information for adopted people and their relatives*, OPCS (booklet).

O'Hagan K (1997) 'The problem of engaging men in child protection work', *British Journal of Social Work*, 27:1, pp 25–42.

Post-Adoption Centre (1990a) *Feeding the Hungry Ghost: A framework for a birth records, intermediary and post-reunion counselling service*, Post-Adoption Centre (Discussion Papers No. 6).

Post-Adoption Centre (1990b) *Groups for Women Who Have Parted with a Child for Adoption*, Post-Adoption Centre (Discussion Papers No. 2).

Rillera M J and Kaplan S (1985) *Co-operative Adoption: A handbook*, (second edition) Triadoption Publications, USA.

Rockel J and Ryburn M (1988) *Adoption Today: Change and choice in New Zealand*, Heinemann Reed, New Zealand.

Ryburn M (ed.) (1994a) *Contested Adoptions: Research, law, policy and practice*, Gower.

Ryburn M (1994b) *Open Adoption: Research, theory and practice*, Avebury.

Sachdev P (1989) *Unlocking the Adoption Files*, D C Heath and Co., Lexington Books, USA.

Shawyer J (1979) *Death by Adoption*, Cicada, New Zealand.

Silverman P R, Campbell L, Patti P and Style C B (1988) 'Reunions between adoptees and birth parents: the birth parents' experience', *Social Work*, 33:6, pp 523–528.

Sorosky A D, Baran A and Pannor R (1984) *The Adoption Triangle: Sealed or open records: how they affect adoptees, birth parents and adoptive parents*, Anchor Books (Original edition: 1978, Anchor Press/Doubleday), USA.

Stanaway E (1996/97) 'Birth parent initiated contact: views and feelings of adult adoptees', *Adoption & Fostering*, 20:4, pp 22–28.

Stogdon P and Hall G (1993) 'Some thoughts on open adoption' in Adcock M, *et al., op. cit.*

Thorpe R (1980) 'The experiences of children and parents living apart: implications and guidelines for practice', in Triseliotis J (ed.), *New Developments in Foster Care and Adoption*, Routledge & Kegan Paul.

Thorpe R (1974) 'The social and psychological situation of the long-term foster child with regard to his natural parents', University of Nottingham, PhD thesis.

Triseliotis J (1973) *In Search of Origins: The experience of adopted people*, Routledge & Kegan Paul.

Triseliotis J (1991) 'Open adoption', 1991 in Mullender A, *op. cit.*

Van Keppel M (1991) 'Birth parents and negotiated adoption agreements', *Adoption & Fostering*, 15:4, pp 81–90.

Vyas I (1993) 'Openness in adoption: some concerns', in Adcock M, *et al., op. cit.*

Ward D (1991) 'Closed adoption – a lifetime loss', in Mullender A, 1991b, *op. cit.*

Webster J (1990) *Webster: An autobiography*, Douglas and McIntyre, Canada.

Wells S (1993a) 'Post-traumatic stress disorder in birthmothers', *Adoption & Fostering*, 17:2, pp 30–32.

Wells S (1993b) 'What do birthmothers want?', *Adoption & Fostering*, 17:4, pp 22–26.

Wells S (1994) *Within Me, Without Me. Adoption: An open and shut case?*, Scarlet Press.

Winkler R C and van Keppel M (1984) *Relinquishing Mothers in Adoption: Their long-term adjustment*, Institute of Family Studies Monograph No. 3, Melbourne, Australia.